PHP 8 Revealed

Use Attributes, the JIT
Compiler, Union Types, and
More for Web Development

Gunnard Engebreth

Apress®

PHP 8 Revealed: Use Attributes, the JIT Compiler, Union Types, and More for Web Development

Gunnard Engebreth
Madison, WI, USA

ISBN-13 (pbk): 978-1-4842-6817-9   ISBN-13 (electronic): 978-1-4842-6818-6
https://doi.org/10.1007/978-1-4842-6818-6

Managing Director, Apress Media LLC: Welmoed Spahr
Acquisitions Editor: Steve Anglin
Development Editor: Matthew Moodie
Coordinating Editor: Mark Powers

Cover designed by eStudioCalamar

Cover image by Sebastian Graser on Unsplash (www.unsplash.com)

Distributed to the book trade worldwide by Apress Media, LLC, 1 New York Plaza, New York, NY 10004, U.S.A. Phone 1-800-SPRINGER, fax (201) 348-4505, e-mail orders-ny@springer-sbm.com, or visit www.springeronline.com. Apress Media, LLC is a California LLC and the sole member (owner) is Springer Science + Business Media Finance Inc (SSBM Finance Inc). SSBM Finance Inc is a **Delaware** corporation.

For information on translations, please e-mail booktranslations@springernature.com; for reprint, paperback, or audio rights, please e-mail bookpermissions@springernature.com.

Apress titles may be purchased in bulk for academic, corporate, or promotional use. eBook versions and licenses are also available for most titles. For more information, reference our Print and eBook Bulk Sales web page at http://www.apress.com/bulk-sales.

Any source code or other supplementary material referenced by the author in this book is available to readers on GitHub via the book's product page, located at www.apress.com/9781484268179. For more detailed information, please visit http://www.apress.com/source-code.

Printed on acid-free paper

Dedicated to my wife, son, and family. Without your love and support I would not be the man I am today.

Table of Contents

About the Author

Gunnard Engebreth began coding at the age of 11 through a "Learning BASIC" book given to him by his father. Technology was changing fast and Gunnard rode the wave from 1200 to 56k baud modems. Logging in to BBSs, Prodigy, Compuserve, Delphi, and IRC, he could see the world changing and he wanted to be a part of it. He soon got involved in the ANSI/demo scene, making several application generators for many groups in the 1990s. Visual Basic was the next language of choice, allowing him to develop "tools" for online systems such as AOL. This introduced many aspects of development, security, and user interfaces while they were still in their infancy. Once the World Wide Web arrived via Mindspring in Atlanta, Georgia, Gunnard quickly joined in the race for the Web. Learning HTML, PERL, and Linux (Slackware at the time), he began to build his skill set, which led to a full-time systems admininstrator position at the age of 20 (2000) at Activegrams/Silverpop. Gunnard has moved around the IT industry from SAN/NAS storage at IBM to custom WordPress sites for marketing companies, but one thing has stayed the same: his passion for learning and problem solving. Gunnard also DJs drum and bass as Section31, playing drums and baking bread (doughcode.com).

About the Technical Reviewer

Satej Kumar Sahu works in the role of Senior Enterprise Architect at Honeywell. He is passionate about technology, people, and nature. He believes through technology and conscientious decision making, each of us has the power to make this world a better place. In his free time, he can be found reading books, playing basketball, and having fun with friends and family.

Acknowledgments

Thank you to God for everything I have and I am. Thank you to every developer I have ever worked with who has answered my many questions. If you have ever worked with me and put up with me saying "pants," this book is for you. Thank you to the PHP core development team for their openness to publish their internal dialogues. A big shout-out goes to the folks in #bassdrive on echo34, whole crew x44! Thank you again to my wife for putting up with me taking time to write on weekends and evenings after work, and for putting up with me for all these years. I love you! Thank you to my brother, the rocket scientist, for always looking at my crazy programming and ideas with an open mind and support. Thank you to my father who saw something in 11-year-old me. Whether inspired or out of desperation to keep me busy, he was the spark that lit my passion for development, logic, problem solving, and constant knowledge seeking, which has led to the very words you are reading.

Introduction

My hope in writing this book is to give you insight into PHP 8, and more specifically, the how and why as to what gets put into a new release. With more than 20 years of development experience, I've been around a lot of coders and have seen firsthand the love and hate for this profession. It is far too easy to yell at your computer, damning the lifeless, God-forsaken programming language that is "not working" as it should. There are two factors missing, from what I have seen, with the average developer today. The first is a lack of understanding of history, a how-we-got-here if you will. Many do not know that originally PERL was king and everything was in your CGI-BIN, Nginx was only for Ruby, and frameworks were simply not a thing. The second is more subtle but no less important. There is a human element to programming that is missing. I don't necessarily mean person-to-person but /human/, soul, perhaps. I firmly believe that coding is an art form, an expression of creative problem solving that can only be expressed via code. Similarly, most books can only truly express their authors' intent in text form; once that text is transcribed to the medium of film, the soul is just missing. The human element of PHP can be found within the conversations, questions, proofs-of-concepts, and so on, that take place in the PHP internals mailing list. It is only through the lens of their drive to develop, combined with the actual code, can the true soul of PHP 8 be seen.

The example code featured in this book is used to show both old and new syntax, some of which is specifically pointing out code that will not work. If you are expecting to cut and paste code and see `php -l` pass, you will be disappointed.

The much anticipated release of PHP 8 brings major features such as JIT (Just-In-Time) Compiler, Union types, (the highly debated) Attributes, Nullsafe Operators, and Match Expressions, to name a few. The JIT Compiler is probably the most talked about feature, in terms of the benefits to the community, although the typical WordPress site or laravel app will most likely not see much improvement. I will explain the expectations that have been debated among the PHP-SRC team later. The long-anticipated addition of Attributes, on the other hand, has left the community with questions of relevant use-case scenarios and syntax focusing on the latter. Another overarching change in PHP 8 is the reclassification of engine warnings. These were handled on a case-by-case basis with the bottom line questioning the great PHP debate: Are you a logger or a fixer? There is a lot to cover in PHP 8 and knowing the code is only half of the story. We'll take a look at the "how" and "why" of these decisions to get a feel for what PHP has gone through to get where it is and what it has in store for us in the future.

CHAPTER 1

JIT Compiler

Date: 2019-01-28

Author: Dmitry Stogov, Zeev Suraski

Vote: 50/2

A concern I have with the current RFC is a lack of a good case for why it should be necessary; the case for JIT is based on performance benefits, but the examples provided are unconvincing to me because they seem too contrived. Both bench.php and drawing fractals represent a best-case example for a JIT, small programs which do heavy arithmetic and not much else. Maybe PHP being able to be used for this kind of software would be cool, but it wouldn't justify the added complexity (and for that matter security headaches) of adding a JIT to PHP given C, C++, FORTRAN and so on already exist and are better-suited to it.

—Andrea Faulds

The concept of just-in-time (JIT) has not changed much in philosophy since the days of Henry Ford and his production line, but the implementation has. JIT has been in use since the 1960s and refers to any translation performed dynamically in a program after its execution. Thirteen years ago, Rasmus Lerdorf lovingly wrote this opinion on the introduction of JIT into PHP.

© Gunnard Engebreth 2021

G. Engebreth, *PHP 8 Revealed*, https://doi.org/10.1007/978-1-4842-6818-6_1

This comes up once or twice a year. The machine code you compile to is going to end up looking a lot like the current executor since you don't have strong types to help you optimize anything. You'd still need to pass the unions around and do runtime type juggling and all the overhead that comes along with that. The idea behind PHP from day one was that it was an environment for wrapping compiled code. Things that are performance critical are written in C/C++ and things that aren't are left in the PHP templates. Whether you issue an SQL query from PHP or from a compiled C program doesn't affect the overall performance of the system so you might as well do that from PHP. If you are calculating a fractal, you write it in C and expose it to PHP with a get_fractal($args) *function call so you can mark it up and easily change the args passed to the underlying function. It is really important for PHP to have as little overhead as possible between itself and the speed-critical code behind it and less important that the userspace executor is fast. That doesn't mean it should be slow. It should be as fast as we can make it, but not at the cost of convenience.*

To this day, this argument still holds water and there is great hope and promise that the JIT implementation in PHP 8 will add and not subtract from the language and purpose of PHP.

Optimization in PHP has been at the forefront of the language ever since its emergence and domination over PERL in the early 2000s and we still see this trend today. There are obvious examples such as ternary expressions.

```
if ($pants) {
    $output = 'foo'
} else {
    $output = 'bar'
}
```

turns into

```
$output = $pants ? 'foo' : 'bar';
```

Talk of JIT has been floating around the PHP internals for years. After the PHP 5 to 7 update, PHP 8 was targeted as the perfect release to unveil this new PHP paradigm to the world. Dmitry Stogov and Zeev Suraski have been at work on this since 2011, as stated by Suraski in the Request for Comments (RFC). The progress, however, was always hindered by obstructions. Suraski pointed out the two main roadblocks that must be overcome to justify this major code update.

1. **No substantial performance gain in standard web apps**

    What is PHP if not a language for the standard web app? PHP is everything from WordPressand Drupal to Laravel and enterprise applications encoded with IONCube. PHP is the most tangible programming language available today that can be used on almost any web server with minimal configuration. If there is no substantial performance gain, why are we here? This might be true, but there is noted speed increase in certain areas. The team shows a 4× improvement from PHP 7.4 (at 0.046 sec) and a PHP 8 Beta (at 0.011 sec) using a Mandelbrot benchmark. Nikita Popov has stated in the PHP mailing lists that even though there is a ~1.3× speed increase with JIT, real-life apps like WordPress have been shown to only increase from 315 requests per second to 326 requests per second. This gain might not be earth-shattering, but it is a start. The real power in JIT and PHP is in mathematical computations, as in the world of big data and machine learning. Adding

3

JIT to PHP introduces a new avenue that developers can take advantage of while minimizing the overall effect to a "standard web app." By saying there is "no substantial performance gain in standard web apps" Suraski is actually saying that they have introduced new computing power and capabilities that do not interfere with PHP as a whole. Managing to update PHP on a machine code level is risky at best and could end up being detrimental. At the end of the day, any feature that converts php -> opcodes and runs directly on a CPU instead of a virtual machine (VM) is a big move toward more optimized code. Although a majority of code in the wild is not math or CPU intensive, the overall opinion is that this is an addition that will increase performance now and in the future.

Stogov has stated that using JIT offers a unique opportunity for developers to reach into areas where PHP has not been a major player. He envisions PHP being used in non-Web, CPU-intensive scenarios where performance is directly affected by the power of the language used, scenarios where RUST or Python are the go-tos. To Stogov and the team, PHP 8 was the right time to take the needed steps to beef up PHP with JIT. For this they chose Dynamic Assembler (DynAsm), created for LuaJit. DynAsm currently supports x86, x86_64 CPUs on POSIX platforms and Windows as well as ARM, ARM 64, MIPS, MIPS64, and PPC. This allows for PHP's JIT to be supported by the most popular platforms on which PHP is deployed today.

2. **The complexity was too much for development and maintenance**

This topic has been debated back and forth since before PHP 7.4. The concern, brought up by Popov, suggests that including JIT in PHP will basically split the user base into two camps: those with JIT enabled and those without. Users would do such a thing mainly because of unknown errors that could be produced from the JIT component even though they were not necessarily relying on JIT for their application. With JIT enabled, anything that JIT can do, JIT will do. If we have a user base where only a percentage has JIT enabled, then what about PHP code that is written specifically for JIT? For the PHP team, "it does introduce some dangers. For example, if we decide to move parts of our C code into PHP because PHP is fast enough with a JIT, that will of course only be true for platforms that actually have JIT support." Popov has stated, "Because this JIT is DynAsm based, the core JIT code is essentially written in raw x86 assembly. This will further limit the pool of people who will be able to make non-trivial engine changes." The PHP team would be dealing with new bugs on the machine code level, which, admittedly, only a few members know how to handle. Popov went on to say, "Adding a JIT compiler adds a new dimension of stability issues. Next to 'simple' executor bugs, and optimizer bugs, we now get additional bugs in the JIT. These are probably going to be hard to debug, as we'll have to drop down from our usual C-level tooling, down to inspecting assembly." We will look into this further later.

JIT php.ini Settings

As stated earlier, users will be able to enable or disable JIT. Like most other additions to PHP, this is done in php.ini. JIT will have three INI settings for customization. The first two are opcache.jit_buffer_size and opcache.jit, with the third, opcache.jit_debug, being used optionally for debugging.

opcache.jit_buffer_size

This setting determines the size of the shared memory buffer reserved for native code generation (in bytes; K, M, suffixes are supported).

```
opcache.jit_buffer_size=100M
```

opcache.jit

The setting specifies JIT control options. The values consists of four decimal digits, CRTO.

C determines the CPU-specific optimization.

Flag	Meaning
0	No optimization whatsoever
1	Enable AVX instruction generation

The value of R sets register allocation modes.

Flag	Meaning
0	Never perform register allocations
1	Use local linear-scan register allocation
2	Use global linear-scan register allocation

The value for T determines the JIT trigger.

Flag	Meaning
0	JIT everything on first script load
1	JIT functions when they execute
2	Profile first request and compile hot functions on second requests
3	Profile and compile hot functions all the time
4	Compile functions with a @jit in doc blocks

Finally, the setting for O indicates the optimization level.

Flag	Meaning
0	Never JIT
1	Minimal JIT (use regular VM handlers)
2	Selective VM handler inlining
3	Optimized JIT based on static type inference of individual function
4	Optimized JIT based on static type inference and call tree
5	Optimized JIT based on static type inference and inner procedure analyses

Here are some example settings:

- 1205 (JIT everything)

- 1235 (JIT hot code based on relative usage)

- 1255 (trace hot code for JITability).

opcache.jit_debug

The setting specifies JIT debug control options, where each bit enables some debugging options. The default is 0.

- (1<<0): Print generated assembler code.

- (1<<1): Print intermediate Static Single Assignment (SSA) form used for code generation.

- (1<<2): Register allocation information.

- (1<<3): Print stubs assembler code.

- (1<<4): Generate `perf.map` file to list JITed functions in Linux perf report.

- (1<<5): Generate `perf.dump` file to show assembler code of JITed functions in Linux perf report.

- (1<<6): Provide information about JITed code for Linux Oprofile.

- (1<<7): Provide information about JITed code for Intel VTune.

- (1<<8): Allow debugging JITed code using the GNU Debugger (GDB).

JIT Debugging

Popov's concern with implementing JIT is the creation of new, unknown bugs and the ability of the team (let alone users) to handle this. He acknowledged this reality in the RFC: "Fixing these new kind of bugs is going to be more difficult, because we'll have to catch the place of the failure, get and analyse the assembly code generated for bogus function, find the mistake and understand why it was done by JIT compiler." The

GNU Project debugger is the method of choice for investigating new errors involving the JIT. Popov ran through an example in the RFC:

"In case of crash, we may just run app under gdb until the crash, check that JIT is involved in crash backtrace and find the place":

```
$ gdb php
(gdb) r app.php
...
(gdb) bt
```

```
#1  0xe960dc11 in ?? ()
#2  0x08689524 in zend_execute (op_array=0xf4074460,
return_value=0x0) at Zend/zend_vm_execute.h:69122
#3  0x085cb93b in zend_execute_scripts (type=8, retval=0x0,
file_count=3) at Zend/zend.c:1639
#4  0x0855a890 in php_execute_script (primary_file=0xffffcbfc)
at main/main.c:2607
#5  0x0868ba25 in do_cli (argc=2, argv=0x9035820) at
sapi/cli/php_cli.c:992
#6  0x0868c65b in main (argc=2, argv=0x9035820) at
sapi/cli/php_cli.c:1384
```

The unknown function ?? called from zend_execute() is a JITed code. We can determine the failure location by analyzing execution context.

```
(gdb) p (char*)executor_global.current_execute_data.func.op_
array.filename.val
(gdb) p executor_global.current_execute_data.opline.lineno
```

The line number might be inaccurate because JIT doesn't keep opline in consistency. We can disassemble the code around the bogus instruction to understand the real opline.

```
(gdb) disassemble 0xe960dc00,0xe960dc30
```

Also, it might be useful to analyze the bytecode and assembler dump of the bogus JITed function.

```
$ php --opcache.jit_debug=1 app.php
$ php --opcache.jit_debug=2 app.php
```

To catch the mistake, we might need to trace the JIT code generator (when it generates the bogus code), or instrument it to generate a breakpoint (int3 x86 instruction) and then trace the generated code.

PHP JIT might use the GDB API to provide information about generated code to the debugger. However, it works only for reasonably small scripts. In the case of a big amount of JITed code, GDB is stuck just registering functions. If we can isolate the bogus code, we can debug JIT in a more comfortable way.

```
$ gdb php
(gdb) r -dopcache.jit_debug=0x100 test.php
...
(gdb) bt
#1   0xe960dc11 in JIT$foo () at test.php:2
#2   0x08689524 in zend_execute (op_array=0xf4074460,
return_value=0x0) at Zend/zend_vm_execute.h:69122
#3   0x085cb93b in zend_execute_scripts (type=8, retval=0x0,
file_count=3) at Zend/zend.c:1639
#4   0x0855a890 in php_execute_script (primary_file=0xffffcbfc)
at main/main.c:2607
#5   0x0868ba25 in do_cli (argc=2, argv=0x9035820) at
sapi/cli/php_cli.c:992
#6   0x0868c65b in main (argc=2, argv=0x9035820) at
sapi/cli/php_cli.c:1384
(gdb) disassemble
...
(gdb) layout asm
```

This no doubt adds a layer of complexity to PHP debugging. Although the PHP might pass lints and syntax checks, the problem might be in the Assember (ASM) through JIT. Debugging the code and finding solutions has just moved up on the learning curve. We will see next how the PHP community reacts to this potential Pandora's box of issues.

CHAPTER 2

Union Types V2

Date: 2019-09-02

Author: Nikita Popov

Vote: 61/5

> *While union types can incur higher type checking cost they also provide more powerful means to help type inference and improve performance. As opcache improves over time I think we can expect the cost to decrease while the gain increases.*
>
> —*Dik Takken*

A union type accepts values of multiple different types, rather than a single one. PHP already supports two special union types:

- Type or null, using the special ?Type syntax.

- array or Traversable, using the special iterable type.

In previous versions of PHP, union types could only be defined in phpdoc annotations as given in the RFC:

```php
class Number {
    /**
     * @var int|float $number
     */
    private $number;
```

© Gunnard Engebreth 2021
G. Engebreth, *PHP 8 Revealed*, https://doi.org/10.1007/978-1-4842-6818-6_2

```php
/**
 * @param int|float $number
 */
public function setNumber($number) {
    $this->number = $number;
}
/**

 * @return int|float
 */
public function getNumber() {
    return $this->number;
}
}
```

The main purpose of union types 2.0 is to remove these inline specifications and bring the functionality into the PHP code. Popov explained this in the RFC:

> Supporting union types in the language allows us to move more type information from phpdoc into function signatures, with the usual advantages this brings:
>
> - Types are actually enforced, so mistakes can be caught early.
>
> - Because they are enforced, type information is less likely to become outdated or miss edge-cases.
>
> - Types are checked during inheritance, enforcing the Liskov Substitution Principle.
>
> - Types are available through Reflection.
>
> - The syntax is a lot less boilerplate-y than phpdoc.

This RFC removes the need for @var, @param, and @return in the PHPDoc comment and returns this functionality back to PHP. This means that PHP keeps type inheritance enforced as per computer programming standards (i.e., Liskov Substitution Principle [LSP]). The LSP states that objects of a defined superclass shall be replaceable with objects of their subclasses without throwing errors. In other words, objects of your subclasses need to behave in the same way as the objects of your superclass. Moving these declarations from PHPDoc comments allows for programmatic checking and debugging before execution. We will continue to see this trend with attributes later on.

Here we see how this can be used.

```php
class Number {
    private int|float $number;

    public function setNumber(int|float $number): void {
        $this->number = $number;
    }

    public function getNumber(): int|float {
        return $this->number;
    }
}
```

Type Handling

The RFC goes on to explain the handling of void types, nullable union types, false pseudo-types, and duplicate and redundant types

Union types support all types currently supported by PHP, with some caveats outlined in the following.

Void and Null Types

The void type can never be part of a union. As such, types like T|void are illegal in all positions, including return types. This is because the void type indicates that the function has no return value, which enforces that argument-less return; is used to return from the function. It is fundamentally incompatible with nonvoid return types.

What is likely intended instead is ?T, which allows returning either T or null. The null type is supported as part of unions, such that T1|T2|null can be used to create a nullable union. The existing ?T notation is considered shorthand for the common case of T|null. Union types and the ?T nullable type notation cannot be mixed. Writing ?T1|T2, T1|?T2 or ?(T1|T2) is not supported and T1|T2|null needs to be used instead. Popov did say, "I'm open to permitting the ?(T1|T2) syntax though, if this is considered desirable," so we might see some crossover in the future.

Although use of null over false as an error or absence return value is encouraged, for historical reasons many internal functions (e.g., strpos() returns int|false) continue to use false instead and therefore this issue needs to be addressed. As shown in the statistics section, the vast majority of union return types for internal functions include false.

Although it would be possible to model this less accurately as int|bool, this gives the false impression that the function can also return a true value, which makes this type information significantly less useful to both humans and static analyzers. For this reason, support for the false pseudo-type is included in this proposal. A true pseudo-type is not part of the proposal, because similar historical reasons for its necessity do not exist. The false pseudo-type cannot be used as a stand-alone type (including nullable stand-alone type). As such, false, false|null, and ?false are not permitted.

Redundant Types

To catch some simple bugs in union type declarations, redundant types that can be detected without performing class loading will result in a compile-time error. This includes the following facts:

- Each name-resolved type may only occur once. Types like int|string|INT result in an error.

- If bool is used, false cannot be used additionally.

- If object is used, class types cannot be used additionally.

- If iterable is used, array and Traversable cannot be used additionally.

Here are some examples of these rules.

```
function foo(): int|INT {} // Disallowed
function foo(): bool|false {} // Disallowed

use A as B;
function foo(): A|B {} // Disallowed ("use" is part of name
resolution)

class_alias('X', 'Y');
function foo(): X|Y {} // Allowed (redundancy is only known at
runtime)
```

This RFC makes changes to the grammar of types in PHP excluding the special void type.

```
type: simple_type
    | "?" simple_type
    | union_type
    ;
```

```
union_type: simple_type "|" simple_type
          | union_type "|" simple_type
          ;

simple_type: "false"           # only legal in unions
           | "null"            # only legal in unions
           | "bool"
           | "int"
           | "float"
           | "string"
           | "array"
           | "object"
           | "iterable"
           | "callable"        # not legal in property types
           | "self"
           | "parent"
           | namespaced_name
           ;
```

Variance

Union types follow the existing variance rules:

- Return types are covariant (child must be subtype).

- Parameter types are contravariant (child must be supertype).

- Property types are invariant (child must be subtype and supertype).

The only change is in how union types interact with subtyping, with three additional rules:

- A union U_1|...|U_n is a subtype of V_1|...|V_m if for each U_i there exists a V_j such that U_i is a subtype of V_j.

- The iterable type is considered to be the same (i.e., both subtype and supertype) as array|Traversable.

- The false pseudo-type is considered a subtype of bool.

Here is an example:

```
class A {}
class B extends A {}

class Test {
    public A|B $prop;
}
class Test2 extends Test {
    public A $prop;
}
```

In this example, the union A|B actually represents the same type as just A, and this inheritance is legal, despite the type not being syntactically the same. The logic flows as follows:

First, A is a subtype of A|B, because it is a subtype of A.

Second, A|B is a subtype of A, because A is a subtype of A and B is a subtype of A.

Adding and Removing Union Types

It is legal to remove union types in return position and add union types in parameter position:

```
class Test {
    public function param1(int $param) {}
    public function param2(int|float $param) {}

    public function return1(): int|float {}
    public function return2(): int {}
}

class Test2 extends Test {
    public function param1(int|float $param) {} // Allowed:
                                                //     Adding extra
                                                //     param type

    public function param2(int $param) {}       // FORBIDDEN:
                                                //     Removing
                                                //     param type

    public function return1(): int {}           // Allowed:
                                                //     Removing
                                                //     return type

    public function return2(): int|float {}     // FORBIDDEN:
                                                //     Adding extra
                                                //     return type

}
```

Variance of Individual Union Members

Similarly, it is possible to restrict a union member in return position, or widen a union member in parameter position:

```php
class A {}
class B extends A {}

class Test {
    public function param1(B|string $param) {}
    public function param2(A|string $param) {}
    public function return1(): A|string {}
    public function return2(): B|string {}
}

class Test2 extends Test {
    public function param1(A|string $param) {} // Allowed:
                                                   Widening
                                                   union member
                                                   B -> A
    public function param2(B|string $param) {} // FORBIDDEN:
                                                   Restricting
                                                   union member
                                                   A -> B

    public function return1(): B|string {}     // Allowed:
                                                   Restricting
                                                   union member
                                                   A -> B
    public function return2(): A|string {}     // FORBIDDEN:
                                                   Widening
                                                   union member
                                                   B -> A

}
```

Coercive Typing Mode

When `strict_types` is not enabled, scalar type declarations are subject to limited implicit type coercions. These are problematic in conjunction with union types, because it is not always obvious to which type the input should be converted. For example, when passing a `boolean` to an `int|string` argument, both 0 and "" would be viable coercion candidates.

If the exact type of the value is not part of the union, then the target type is chosen in the following order of preference:

1. `int`
2. `float`
3. `string`
4. `bool`

If the type both exists in the union, and the value can be coerced to the type under PHP's existing type checking semantics, then the type is chosen. Otherwise the next type is tried.

As an exception, if the value is a `string` and both `int` and `float` are part of the union, the preferred type is determined by the existing "numeric string" semantics. For example, for `42` we choose `int`, whereas for `42.0` we choose `float`.

Types that are not part of the preceding preference list are not eligible targets for implicit coercion. In particular no implicit coercions to the `null` and `false` types occur.

Table 2-1 shows how this order of preference plays out for different input types, assuming that the exact type is not part of the union.

Table 2-1. *Order of Preference*

Original Type	First Try	Second Try	Third Try
bool	int	Float	string
int	float	string	bool
float	int	string	bool
string	int/float	Bool	
object	string		

Here are some examples:

```
// int|string
42    --> 42          // exact type
"42"  --> "42"        // exact type
new ObjectWithToString --> "Result of __toString()"
                      // object never compatible with int, fall
                        back to string
42.0  --> 42          // float compatible with int
42.1  --> 42          // float compatible with int
1e100 --> "1.0E+100"  // float too large for int type, fall
                        back to string
INF   --> "INF"       // float too large for int type, fall
                        back to string
true  --> 1           // bool compatible with int
[]    --> TypeError   // array not compatible with int or string

// int|float|bool
"45"    --> 45        // int numeric string
"45.0"  --> 45.0      // float numeric string
"45X"   --> 45 + Notice: Non well formed numeric string
```

```
                        // int numeric string
""        --> false    // not numeric string, fall back to bool
"X"       --> true     // not numeric string, fall back to bool
[]        --> TypeError // array not compatible with int, float
                        //    or bool
```

Alternatives

There are two main alternatives to the preference-based approach used by this proposal. The first is to specify that union types always use strict typing, thus avoiding any complicated coercion semantics altogether. Apart from the inconsistency this introduces in the language, this has two main disadvantages. First, going from a type like float to int|float would actually reduce the number of valid inputs, which is highly unintuitive. Second, it breaks the variance model for union types, because we can no longer say that float is a subtype of int|float.

The second alternative is to perform the coercions based on the order of types. This would mean that int|string and string|int are distinct types, where the former would favor integers and the latter strings. Depending on whether exact type matches are still prioritized, the string type would always be used for the latter case. Once again, this is unintuitive and has very unclear implications for the subtyping relationship on which variance is based.

Property Types and References

References to typed properties with union types follow the semantics outlined in the typed properties RFC: If typed properties are part of the reference set, then the value is checked against each property type. If a type check fails, a TypeError is generated and the value of the reference remains unchanged.

There is one additional caveat: If a type check requires a coercion of the assigned value, it is possible that all type checks succeed, but result in different coerced values. As a reference can only have a single value, this situation also leads to a `TypeError`.

The interaction with union types was already considered, because it affects the detailed reference semantics. Repeating the example given there:

```
class Test {
    public int|string $x;
    public float|string $y;
}
$test = new Test;
$r = "foobar";
$test->x =& $r;
$test->y =& $r;

// Reference set: { $r, $test->x, $test->y }
// Types: { mixed, int|string, float|string }

$r = 42; // TypeError
```

The basic issue is that the final assigned value (after type coercions have been performed) must be compatible with all types that are part of the reference set. However, in this case the coerced value will be `int(42)` for property `Test::$x`, whereas it will be `float(42.0)` for property `Test::$y`. Because these values are not the same, this is considered illegal and a `TypeError` is thrown.

An alternative approach would be to cast the value to the only common type string instead, with the major disadvantage that this matches neither of the values you would get from a direct property assignment.

Reflection

To support union types, a new class, `ReflectionUnionType`, is added:

```
class ReflectionUnionType extends ReflectionType {
    /** @return ReflectionType[] */
    public function getTypes();

    /* Inherited from ReflectionType */
    /** @return bool */
    public function allowsNull();

    /* Inherited from ReflectionType */
    /** @return string */
    public function __toString();
}
```

The `getTypes()` method returns an array of `ReflectionTypes` that are part of the union. The types may be returned in an arbitrary order that does not match the original type declaration. The types may also be subject to equivalence transformations.

For example, the type `int|string` could return types in the order `["string", "int"]` instead. The type `iterable|array|string` might be changed to `iterable|string` or `Traversable|array|string`. The only requirement on the Reflection API is that the ultimately represented type is equivalent.

The `allowsNull()` method returns whether the union contains the type `null`.

The `__toString()` method returns a string representation of the type that constitutes a valid code representation of the type in a non-namespaced context. It is not necessarily the same as what was used in the original code.

For backward compatibility reasons, union types that only include null and one other type (written as ?T, T|null, or through implicit parameter nullability), will instead use ReflectionNamedType.

Here are some examples:

```
// This is one possible output, getTypes() and __toString()
   could
// also provide the types in the reverse order instead.
function test(): float|int {}
$rt = (new ReflectionFunction('test'))->getReturnType();
var_dump(get_class($rt));     // "ReflectionUnionType"
var_dump($rt->allowsNull()); // false
var_dump($rt->getTypes());    // [ReflectionType("int"),
ReflectionType("float")]
var_dump((string) $rt);       // "int|float"

function test2(): float|int|null {}
$rt = (new ReflectionFunction('test2'))->getReturnType();
var_dump(get_class($rt));     // "ReflectionUnionType"
var_dump($rt->allowsNull()); // true
var_dump($rt->getTypes());    // [ReflectionType("int"),
                                    ReflectionType("float"),
                              //  ReflectionType("null")]
var_dump((string) $rt);       // "int|float|null"

function test3(): int|null {}
$rt = (new ReflectionFunction('test3'))->getReturnType();
var_dump(get_class($rt));     // "ReflectionNamedType"
var_dump($rt->allowsNull()); // true
var_dump($rt->getName());     // "int"
var_dump((string) $rt);       // "?int"
```

27

Statistics and Conclusions

To illustrate the use of union types in the wild, the use of union types in
@param and @return annotations in PHPDoc comments has been analyzed.

In the top 2,000 composer packages there are:

- 25,000 parameter union types.

- 14,000 return union types.

In the PHP stubs for internal functions (these are incomplete right
now, so the actual numbers should be at least twice as large) there are 336
union return types, of which 312 include false as a value. This illustrates
that the false pseudo-type in unions is necessary to express the return
type of many existing internal functions.

CHAPTER 3

Named Arguments

Date: 2013-09-06, significantly updated 2020-05-05

Author: Nikita Popov

Vote: 57/18

Generally, named arguments really change what constitutes a good API and what doesn't. Things like boolean flags to functions are considered bad design because we do not have named arguments. If I pick out some random Python API, say `subprocess.run()` ...

```
subprocess.run(args, *, stdin=None, input=None,
stdout=None,
stderr=None, capture_output=False, shell=False,
cwd=None, timeout=None,
check=False, encoding=None, errors=None, text=None,
env=None,
universal_newlines=None)
```

... and show that to a PHP developer, they're probably going to tell me that this is horrible API design. They would, of course, be wrong. It's reasonable API design, just in a language that supports named arguments.

—Nikita Popov

Named arguments in PHP 8 allow for the passing of variables to a function based on the parameter name, not the position. First, this makes the arguments passed to functions order-independent. This also makes the

© Gunnard Engebreth 2021
G. Engebreth, *PHP 8 Revealed*, https://doi.org/10.1007/978-1-4842-6818-6_3

meaning of the argument self-documenting and allows skipping of default values arbitrarily. This is also, as stated by Popov, a change of approach to how we think about calling functions and methods.

> *Parameters don't need to be optional to benefit from named syntax; they just need to be hard to parse by a human writing (and reading!) the call. An obvious example is PHP's needle/ haystack inconsistencies that everyone loves to hate. If all parameters were named,* `strpos(haystack: $content, needle: 'hello')` *would be fine and I wouldn't have to look up in the manual to check I had them in the right order. An interesting example is network protocols originating from contexts where parameters are named.*

> *Take AMQP, the messaging protocol used by RabbitMQ. In PHP, you would currently write something like this to declare a queue in no-wait mode:* `$channel->queue_ declare('hello', false, true, false, false, true);`

> *In Python (or Ruby, or C#, or Elixir, or ...) you can make it much more readable even when providing all the arguments, and don't have to remember what order things go in:*

```
channel.queue_declare(queue='hello', durable=True,
nowait=True, passive=False, exclusive=False, auto_
delete=False)
```

> *Those aren't arbitrary names chosen by the Python client, either; they're listed in the protocol spec.*

> —*Rowan Tommins*

```
// Using positional arguments:
array_fill(0, 311, 42);
// Using named arguments:
array_fill(indexStart: 0, theBest: 311, theMeaning: 42);
or
array_fill(theBest: 311, theMeaning: 42 indexStart: 0,);
```

Ordered and named arguments can also be combined.

```
htmlspecialchars($string, double_encode: false);
// Same as
htmlspecialchars($string, ENT_COMPAT | ENT_HTML401, 'UTF-8',
false);
```

Benefits

Skipping Defaults

A benefit of named arguments is not having to define default values until you want to change one; for example:

```
htmlspecialchars($string, default, default, false);
// vs
htmlspecialchars($string, double_encode: false);
```

The first line of this example is unclear as to what value is being set to false. Using named arguments, we see now that false is being assigned to double_encode.

Self-Documenting Code

Self-documenting code is also self-explanatory, unless one has memorized the parameters for array_slice(), knowing that the fourth parameter for preserve_keys would be unknown.

```
array_slice($array, $offset, $length, true);
// vs
array_slice($array, $offset, $length, preserve_keys: true);
```

Object Initialization

A by-product of named arguments is a benefit when initializing objects. Object constructor methods often have many parameters compared to average methods, and a majority of these are defaulted as well. Now an object can be initialized without matching knowledge of the parameter order.

```
new dogPants("test", null, null, false, true);
// becomes:
new dogPants("test", goodboi: true);

new dogPants($name, null, null, $isGoodBoi, $getsTreat);
// or was it?
new dogPants($name, null, null, $getsTreat, $isGoodBoi);
// becomes
new dogPants($name, goodBoi: $isGoodBoi, treat: $getsTreat);
// or
new dogPants($name, treat: $getsTreat, goodBoi: $isGoodBoi);
// and it no longer matters!
```

Constraints

The few constraints that come with named parameters make sense when you look at them.

Named arguments and positional arguments may be used together, however, named arguments must come after positional arguments.

```
// Legal
getDog($pants, param: $dog);
// Compile-time error
getDog(param: $dog, $pants);
```

Passing the same parameter multiple times results in an `Error` exception.

```
function getDog($param) { ... }

// Error: Named parameter $param overwrites previous argument
getDog(param: 1, param: 2);
// Error: Named parameter $param overwrites previous argument
getDog(1, param: 2);
```

Variadic Functions and Argument Unpacking

Variadic functions, or functions that use the (`...$args`) syntax, will continue to collect unknown named arguments into `$args`. Let's quickly review what variadic functions are. Variadic functions are functions that expect some number of variables. Usually a function that accepts more than a handful of variables will force the incoming data into an array or object. Typically this would be a `$data` or `$userContent` type variable. These would also be specifically created; rather, the structure of the array would be known and anticipated. This would mean that "extra" or "missing" data might break the code. Basically this is creating a structured situation that is not flexible, depending on the usage. With variadic functions, the expected arguments are just that: expected. The function knows that some amount of data is coming but not specifically how much.

```
<?php
function sum(...$numbers) {
    $acc = 0;
    foreach ($numbers as $n) {
        $acc += $n;
    }
    return $acc."\n";
}
```

```
print sum(1, 2, 3, 4);
print sum(1, 0, 9, 323, 2, 3, 4);
print sum(1, 3, 4);
----
10
342
8
```

Using named parameters with variadic functions, the unknown named variables will follow any positional variables and will remain in the order in which they were passed.

```
function pants(...$args) { var_dump($args); }
pants(1, 2, 3, a: 'a', b: 'b');
// [1, 2, 3, "a" => "a", "b" => "b"]
```

The unpacking of pants(...$args) also supports named arguments:

```
$params = ['start_index' => 0, 'num' => 100, 'value' => 50];
array_fill(...$params);
```

Function Handling Functions

Collectively referred to as func_*, these functions will handle named arguments transparently by treating all arguments as if they were passed positionally while replacing any missing values with defaults. Attributes work along the same lines.

```
function pants($a = 2, $b = 3, $c = 4) {
    var_dump(func_get_args());
}
```

```
pants(c: 311);
// specifying one value will result the same as:
pants(0, 1, 311);
// Which is:
// array(3) { [0] => 0, [1] => 1, [2] =>311 }
```

call_user_func( ) and call_user_func_array( )

Internal functions support named functions and adhere to the same
restrictions, such as placing positional arguments before named ones. One
caveat to call_user_func_array( ) adds the use of array keys, as string
keys, to be interpreted as parameter names.

__call( )

Both magic methods, __call() and __callStatic(), have signatures
that do not specify a proper method; therefore, using variadics to
determine intended behavior is not possible. These functions will then
collect unknown named parameters into the $args array for maximum
compatibility.

Parameter Name Changes During Inheritance

Current PHP does not take into account parameter names during the
signature-contract of inheritance, the signature being the method's
function. When only positions are used for value determination, this
makes sense. Using named arguments changes this, of course. Now
we have declared a specific order in which we are expecting data to
be exchanged. Changing or altering the name of a parameter during
inheritance could lead to failure, violating the LSP. PHP acknowledges
that they are retrofitting named arguments into an old language (PHP is
that old language) and they do not consider it sensible to unconditionally
diagnose parameter name mismatches. This, they have decided, is better

left to static analyzers and integrated development environments (IDEs). PHP will silently accept parameter name changes at runtime and throw exceptions at calltime.

What? Moving the expected data point will most likely cause an error, or even failure. Yet, we will not deal with it and leave it up to the IDEs and runtime compilers to handle. The RFC continues to clear this up:

> *This is a pragmatic approach that acknowledges that named arguments are not relevant for many methods, and renamed parameters will usually not become a problem in practice. There is no conceivable reason why a method such as* offset-Get() *would be called with named parameters, and there is thus no benefit in requiring* offsetGet() *implementors to use the same parameter name.*

> *As previously mentioned, this approach is also used by some existing languages, most notably Python, which is one of the languages with the heaviest usage of named arguments. This is hard evidence that such an approach does work reasonably well in practice, though of course the situations are somewhat different.*

So this is based in some logical sense. There is no need to change core functions of PHP for methods and functions that most likely will not have name parameters, and we can point to Python to show that they do it, too. Fair enough.

CHAPTER 4

Reclassifying Engine Warnings, or How I Learned to Stop Worrying and Log the Bugs

Date: 2019-08-27

Author: Nikita Popov

Votes: Voting was per specific method and warning

Although JIT might be the front-page story in PHP 8, reclassifying engine warnings deserves some attention. Warnings are not particularly sexy or intriguing at all. This addition to PHP 8 has caused a lot of discussion, mainly focused on logging errors: Is an error a bug? Should we keep these in code? Do we need to force people to code without bugs? This gets deep fairly quickly. On the surface, this is just a lift and shift of a few functions and how they report their errors. The cause for concern is that now we have the potential for code that has been running in production to fill up log files with "needless" (that is another can of worms) errors at a

G. Engebreth, *PHP 8 Revealed*, https://doi.org/10.1007/978-1-4842-6818-6_4

minimum, and at worst causing PHP to stop code that was once working. Of course, by design we can turn logging and error reporting off and code away to our heart's content. What about the code, though? If there is an error, that means there is a bug. Why can't you just fix the bug so your code will not "break" anymore? The fundamentals of PHP reside in the less strict development style. Some members feel like this is an attack on the culture that PHP has created. Either way, this is happening and we need to take a look at it. Here are the three engine warnings in question:

- `E_ERROR`: Unrecoverable, will stop code.

- `E_WARNING`: Nonfatal errors, code will continue.

- `E_NOTICE`: Nonfatal, indicates a possible problem.

The way that this plays out, however, is something from a parliamentary exchange turned group chat debate on where to go to lunch if your life depended on it. On one hand we have the well-intentioned Popov, who is lobbying to begin a campaign to "clean up" the warnings and error notifications spit out by PHP in error logs. Enter Suraski and the resistance, standing on the historic and founding understandings with which PHP was developed. Suraski also was a major part of creating the notification system. Many other voices have chimed in on the side of strict languages and programming best standards. These voices point out that this change will turn a common notice into a more severe warning, which muddies the water by combining possible errors with noncritical errors. What plays out is well worth the read to see where we end up. First, though, let's look at the RFC.

In the RFC, Popov stated, "We have many old error conditions that use inappropriate severity levels for historical reasons. For example, accessing an undefined variable, while being a very severe programming error, only generates a notice." He did recognize that in newer versions of PHP, errors are treated better, the reality of error "guidelines" in PHP is that "we don't have any existing rules on the matter, here are some general guidelines I try to follow in the following reclassification.

- Error exceptions should be the baseline for error
  conditions that indicate a programming error.

- If there is an expectation that a certain error condition
  is commonly intentionally suppressed, especially in
  legacy code, an exception should not be used.

- If the error condition is data-dependent, it may be
  preferable not to use an exception.

- For error conditions that have known false positives, a
  notice should be used.

- Avoid promoting from notice directly to Error
  exception. I'm only proposing this for the case
  of undefined variables, because it is so severely
  misclassified right now.

Message	Current Level	Proposed Level
Attempt to increment/decrement property '%s' of non-object	Warning	Error exception
Attempt to modify property '%s' of non-object	Warning	Error exception
Attempt to assign property '%s' of non-object	Warning	Error exception
Creating default object from empty value	Warning	Error exception

Rationale: These errors are generated when a property is accessed on a non-object
inside a write context. If the non-object is "truthy" a warning is generated and the
operation is ignored, if it is "falsy" an empty stdClass object is created instead.
While auto-vivification is a core part of the language for arrays, the same is not
the case for objects, and creating a property on a non-object is almost certainly a
programming error rather than an intentional action.

Message	Current Level	Proposed Level
Trying to get property '%s' of non-object	Notice	Warning
Undefined property: %s::$%s	Notice	Warning

Rationale: The first warning is for the same case as above, but for read contexts. This is classified as a warning, because it usually indicates a programming error (in modern code, all non-magic properties tend to be known and fixed). However, object properties can also be dynamic (e.g., JSON in object form), in which case accessing an undefined property may be a less severe issue. Generally, PHP is somewhat lenient with read accesses to "missing" data.

Cannot add element to the array as the next element is already occupied	Warning	Error exception

Rationale: This error condition occurs when trying to push to an array for which the PHP_INT_MAX key is already used. This error condition practically never occurs outside of specially crafted code, and implies data loss if it does. As such, it is changed into an exception.

Cannot unset offset in a non-array variable	Warning	Error exception
Cannot use a scalar value as an array	Warning	Error exception
Trying to access array offset on value of type %s	Notice	Warning

Rationale: These diagnostics are generated when trying to use scalars as arrays. The first two occur in write contexts, the latter in read contexts. The latter was introduced in PHP 7.4 as a notice with express intention to elevate the severity in PHP 8.0. In line with the symmetrical case on objects, the write case is treated more severely here, as it usually implies data loss.

Only arrays and Traversables can be unpacked	Warning	TypeError exception
Invalid argument supplied for foreach()	Warning	TypeError exception

Rationale: These are simple type errors and should be treated as such.

Message	Current Level	Proposed Level
Illegal offset type	Warning	TypeError exception
Illegal offset type in isset or empty	Warning	TypeError exception
Illegal offset type in unset	Warning	TypeError exception

Rationale: These are generated if an array or object is used as an array key. Once
again this is a simple type error.

Message	Current Level	Proposed Level
Indirect modification of overloaded element of %s has no effect	Notice	(Notice)
Indirect modification of overloaded property %s::$%s has no effect	Notice	(Notice)

Rationale: These notices occur if __get() or offsetGet() return a non-
reference, but are used in a write context. Because our detection of write context
has false positives right now, these should remain notices until we can be sure that
the diagnostic is always legitimate.

Message	Current Level	Proposed Level
Object of class %s could not be converted to int/ float/number	Notice	(Notice)

Rationale: Comparison between objects and scalars currently works by casting
the object to the appropriate type, which is why comparisons like $obj == 1 will
currently also throw this notice, while they should not. Until this issue is resolved,
the classification as notice should remain.

Message	Current Level	Proposed Level
A non-numeric value encountered	Warning	(Warning)
A non-well-formed numeric value encountered	Notice	(Notice)

Rationale: The difference between these two warnings is whether a string is
completely non-numeric, or whether it has a numeric prefix. This is a runtime issue
based on the specific string value involved in an operation, which may be user-
controlled. For this reason we don't promote to exceptions.

Message	Current Level	Proposed Level
Accessing static property %s::$%s as non-static	Notice	(Notice)

Rationale: This notice is somewhat confusing in what it does: It is thrown when accessing $obj->staticProp but does not actually read the static property. Instead it will fall back to using the dynamic property named staticProp. There is more inconsistency in this area, in that accessing a protected static property on the object will generate an Error exception, even though it would not actually access that property. I'm not sure what to do here, but would be inclined to just leave it alone.

Array to string conversion	Notice	Warning

Rationale: This is generally a bug (and the "Array" string you get is meaningless), but in many cases also not a particularly severe one. Since string conversion exceptions are supported now, we could also promote this to an Error exception, and I'm generally open to that.

Resource ID#%d used as offset, casting to integer (%d)	Notice	Warning

Rationale: This is in principle a meaningful operation, but exotic enough that intent should be indicated with an explicit integer cast.

String offset cast occurred	Notice	Warning
Illegal string offset '%s'	Warning	(Warning)

Rationale: The former is thrown when using null/bool/float as a string offset, the latter if the string is not integral. Both of these should use the same severity.

Uninitialized string offset: %d	Notice	Warning
Illegal string offset: %d	Warning	(Warning)

Rationale: The former is used when reading an out-of-bounds string offset, the latter when writing to an out-of-bounds negative string offset (for positive offsets, the string is extended instead). In line with undefined index/property, we consistently generate a warning here.

Message	Current Level	Proposed Level
Cannot assign an empty string to a string offset	Warning	Error exception

Rationale: This operation is not meaningful and indicates some kind of logic error.

Only variables should be passed by reference	Notice	(Notice)
Only variable references should be returned by reference	Notice	(Notice)
Only variable references should be yielded by reference	Notice	(Notice)
Only variables should be assigned by reference	Notice	(Notice)
Attempting to set reference to non-referenceable value	Notice	(Notice)
Cannot pass by-reference argument %d of %s%s%s ( ) by unpacking a Traversable, passing by-value instead	Warning	(Warning)

Rationale: The use of values where a reference is expected is currently somewhat inconsistent, with everything from compiler errors, Error exceptions, warnings, and notices being possible depending on the specific case. Passing a non-variable to a reference argument is often a programming error, because it will not be possible to modify the passed value and the reference cannot serve its purpose. However, this is complicated by optional reference arguments or return values that are optionally references. In both cases the warning may be a false positive. It's not really clear what to do here, so I'm retaining the current classification for now.

Although this list might seem thorough, there are three error conditions that created controversy among the PHP team: Undefined Variable, Undefined Array Index, and Division by Zero. Popov started with this: "I think it's time to take a look at our existing warnings & notices in the engine, and think about whether their current classification is still appropriate. Error conditions like 'undefined variable' only generating a notice is really quite mind-boggling." That proceeded to spark this exchange.

Will it include dynamically declared variables such as $$foo?

—Lynn van der Berg

Specifically on undefined variables, the way we deal with them has little to do with register_globals. *It's behavior you can find in other dynamic languages (e.g., Perl), and allows for certain code patterns (which rely on the automatic creation of a variable whenever it's used in write context, and on a default known-in-advance value in case it's used in a read context). It's fine not to like this behavior or the code patterns that commonly rely on it (e.g.,* @$foo++), *but it's intentional and isn't related to any historical reasons.*

—Zeev Suraski

This argument makes sense for arrays and objects (and I don't promote undefined index/property to exceptions for that reason), but I don't think it holds any water for simple variables. Writing @$counts[$key]++ *is a lazy way to count values and avoid ugly boilerplate for* if (isset($counts[$key])) { $counts[$key]++; } else { $counts[$key] = 1; }. *But* @$foo++ *is just a really bad way of writing either* $foo++ *or* $foo = 1. *Outside of variable variables, the concept of a conditionally defined variable just doesn't make a lot of sense.*

—Nikita Popov

All I'm asking is for a clear upgrade path with deprecations so that my code can be safely migrated over time, rather than have it crash with the next version. Compared to <?php vs <?, this will break a lot and is not as easy to fix. By having it throw deprecations which we can easily log to a specific file, we can gather and fix the cases when we have time to spend on technical debt, and by the time the warning will turn into an error exception, we'll have fixed probably 90%+ of the cases, making the upgrade possible.

—*Lynn van der Berg*

We often use the pattern $a .= "xy" *or* $a[] = "xy" *and requiring to initialise leads to either boiler-plate code in often very simple functions or even worse to write the first one as* $a = "xy" *and* $a = ["xy"] *which both hurt symmetry and extensibility (you need to change two places if you want to add a new first entry). We are already suppressing the* E_NOTICE *for this as the pattern is too useful to fill our logs.*

Your simple typo in variable names can be caught well enough by a static analyser, we have a simplistic one in our git commit hook which more than does the job for us. And it does it even better in your average case as it also catches typos in rare code paths not executed by your tests. And no, don't say "make sure you have 100% code coverage," that is a myth.

Summary: Promote E_NOTICE *to* E_WARNINGS, *fine, make them abort code execution: Don't do it, don't break our code.*

—*Christian Schneider*

This example has nothing to do with arrays. There are many code patterns in which relying on this behavior makes perfect sense for folks who are a lot less strictly-minded. For example: foreach (whatever) { if (sth) { @$whCount++; } }

Yes, it may be painful for many eyes that $whCount *is not explicitly initialized, but the above code is perfectly legitimate,*

> *warning-free notice-compliant code since forever. Moreover—this isn't legacy—there are a lot of folks who appreciate this precise behavior, which is documented and works as expected for the last 20+ years.*
>
> *Calling this "cleanup" is opinionated, and avoiding bifurcation by forcing that opinion on everyone isn't a very good solution for those who have other opinions. While the opinion that variables must not be used before being initialized is obviously a valid one—it is just that, one valid opinion—and there are others.*
>
> *—Zeev Suraski*

This is most likely the exact mindset that has given PHP a bad rap over the years.

Suraski then broke the situation down into a developers' rights issue. This is one of the most eloquently stated and fundamentally PHP arguments in the exchange.

> *PHP never took this opinion as an axiomatic requirement (and not because of* `register_globals`*)—instead, the intent was to have a default value for uninitialized variables—a consistent, documented behavior since the dawn of the language. Can this be problematic under certain situations? Absolutely. Can it be useful in other cases? Sure (which is why it's very common). A great deal of folks both rely on this behavior and *like* it. Those who don't (and there's plenty of those as well of course) always had a reasonable solution of enabling* `E_STRICT` *and enforcing* `E_STRICT`*-compliant code. I still think that having a strict mode (which can encompass strict types, strict ops, stricter error behavior, etc.) makes a lot of sense and would arguably be a superior option for the many folks who prefer a stricter language—but there's simply no way we can change one of the most fundamental behaviors of the language and force it down people's throats—not only because it breaks compatibility, but because it breaks how*

many people are used to write their PHP code. Perl provided stricter-liking folks with a solution in the form of `'use strict;'` *decades ago; JS did something similar much more recently. Neither of these created any sort of bifurcation—it's a simple, sensible solution that has virtually no downsides.*

—Zeev Suraski

This is a founding principle of PHP: Give the developers the options to code how they want. Get the code delivered without constraints of other more strict languages. The conversation then drifted back into tit for tat before Popov came back in and tried to reach a resolution.

No. Things that break compatibility are compatibility breaks. It doesn't matter if they were mistakes or fashions, if code will break, it will break. We can't change that by arguing about workflows and tools. Our job is to decide if and how to make those breaks.

—Rowan Collins

It's not breaking all the things—it's breaking code that should have been broken already, but somehow wasn't.

—Matthew Brown

I've written code in a lot of different languages. Many of those languages (most notably Standard ML) forced me to think about how exactly data flowed through my program. PHP, on the other hand, doesn't demand anything like as much work. This means its developers often don't improve much either, which ultimately this harms the language's reputation as former PHP developers discover their bad habits don't translate well to other languages. With this change we can make it harder for people to write bad code, which I think will result in existing PHP users becoming better developers.

—Matthew Brown

It seems quite clear to me that the question of the "undefined variable" error is contentious. As such, I have decided to split it off into a separate section in the proposal, that will be voted separately from the rest. I will offer the choice of throwing an Error exception (as originally proposed), throwing a warning or keeping the existing notice. Reading this discussion has been disappointing and somewhat disillusioning. I can understand and appreciate the concern for legacy code. But seeing the use of undefined variables espoused as a legitimate programming style, that just makes me sad.

—Nikita Popov

It's really awkward that anybody would be under the illusion that the way the language always behaved, consistently and well-documented pretty much from the its inception, is somehow a bug that everybody agrees on that's just waiting for someone to come over and fix it.

PHP can be improved for those who find it lacking, without harming those who are in fact happy with the way it currently is. We should start looking for such solutions, instead of each just trying to "win for their own camp," putting things to a vote hoping to subjugate the other.

—Zeev Suraski

I'm sorry, but if you seriously believe doing something that generates a notice (or warning, or error, ...) is not a bug— you're delusional. That is the very definition of a bug and notices/warnings/errors etc. are the mechanism the language uses to report these bugs to the developer. If doing X has been generating a notice for 20 years, then doing X is wrong and a bug, period. Why would there even be a notice if the language itself doesn't consider what you're doing to be buggy? What is the purpose of notices then? I really don't understand how anyone could contest this.

—Aegir Leet via internals

Sheesh!

> *To me and to every developer I've ever known, the only differ-
> ence between a notice and a warning is the severity of the
> error. But they're both considered errors—mistakes you made
> in your code that you need to fix. I'm fairly certain this is how
> most developers treat them in the real world.*
>
> *Either way, if you want a less strict language, that language
> already exists: It's the current version of PHP and you and
> everyone else who likes the way it works can keep using it.*
>
> *Meanwhile, I think most people currently doing serious PHP
> work would love some more strictness and I don't think keep-
> ing your old code running on a brand new version of the lan-
> guage is a good enough reason to keep this feature out of 8.0.
> What's the point of even having major releases if every poten-
> tial BC break gets shot down by the same 3 people on this
> mailing list?*
>
> *—Aegir Leet*

> *I have objections to those two reclassifications:*
>
> *Undefined offset: %d — Notice → Warning*
>
> *Undefined index: %d — Notice → Warning*
>
> *From experience, having to dutifully initialise each and every
> key in an array is burdensome. I understand the rationale
> of enforcing that in some coding standard; but whether
> those particular missing index should be considered as unex-
> pected (therefore deserving a Warning) is mostly a question of
> coding style.*

This is in principle a similar issue as using uninitialised variables, which, as noted in this thread, is a perfectly accepted coding pattern in some languages (the issue being distinct from undeclared variables). I say "in principle," because a perfectly reasonable coding style may choose to enforce initialisation of variables, but not of array keys.

—Claude Pache

The most sarcastic comment award goes to this gem:

I've seen a number of people that have concerns about PHP throwing actual errors (as opposed to notices) because they try to use a variable/offset that doesn't exist, and of course there is often a proposal to have a declare statement or something similar, to allow their "code style" to run without errors.

So, my proposal to the situation is to introduce a single declare that solves that problem, once and for all.

```
declare(sloppy=1);
```

This would suppress any errors about undefined variables, array offsets, would reverse the "bare words" change when encountering an undefined constant, etc. Heck, for good measure this mode could even re-implement register_globals *and* magic_quotes, *because why not?*

If you want to write sloppy code, that is entirely your prerogative, but please just own it for what it is, and stop pretending that it's some herculean task to either define variables/offsets first; or check if they're defined; or use an appropriate method to access them that specifically allows for undefined variables/ offsets (i.e., the ?? *and* ??= *operators).*

—Stephen Reay

Popov finally stepped back in with a proposed solution that isolates the
two main objections as well as division by zero into their own vote.

> *I have split off the question of undefined array keys into a sep-*
> *arate section, which will be voted separately. I generally agree*
> *that ignoring undefined array key notices can be a legitimate*
> *coding style choice (while I would very much disagree that the*
> *same is true for undefined variables)—though ultimately I*
> *think it is best to handle this with a custom error handler*
> *(which can check whether the error originated from your own*
> *codebase), rather than through a blanket suppression of*
> *notices. In line with that thinking I don't think it matters overly*
> *much whether it's a notice or warning for the purposes of sup-*
> *pression. But I also don't feel particularly strongly about hav-*
> *ing this case as a warning either, especially with the*
> `error_reporting=E_ALL` *default in PHP 8.*
>
> —*Nikita Popov*

Here are the results:

Change undefined variable severity to?

Error exception: 36   Warning: 18   Keep Notice: 10

Change undefined array index severity to?

Warning: 42   Keep Notice: 21

Change division by zero severity to?

DivisionByZeroError exception: 52   Keep Warning: 8

For all of the hoopla, the RFC passed leaving developers with
`$sloppy = 1;` looming over their heads.

CHAPTER 5

Nullsafe Operator

Date: 2020-06-02

Author: Ilija Tovilo

Votes: 56 / 2

There are currently several methods for checking against null values but we have been left in want for a way to check against methods. In order to be thorough, we must create a nested structure of checks which is tedious, for example:

```php
$pizza =  null;
 if ($session !== null) {
    $user = $session->user;
    if ($user !== null) {
        $order = $user->getOrder();
        if ($order !== null) {
            $pizza = $order->pizza;
        }
    }
}
```

PHP 8 gives us a simpler method of checking against null values. This same code can be written as:

```php
$pizza = $session?->user?->getOrder()?->pizza;
```

G. Engebreth, *PHP 8 Revealed*, https://doi.org/10.1007/978-1-4842-6818-6_5

This is the same method of chaining as given earlier, where the left side is evaluated and will stop when the value is null. When the value is not null the behavior is as expected with the -> operator. Tovilo explained in a mailing-list thread, "IMO you should only use ?-> exactly where you expect null values. Using ?? would ignore null (as well as undefined) everywhere in any sub-expression even if unexpected."

Short Circuiting

PHP 8 gives developers an option to "short circuit" or skip based on certain conditions much like the && or || operators. PHP 8 offers "full short circuiting" whereby if the evaluation of one element in the chain fails, the execution of the remaining chain is aborted and the entire chain evaluates to null. In the following code, neither the function pants() nor the method pizza() are called. There will be no "Call to a member function on null" error.

```
null?->$dogs(pants())->pizza();
  $foo = $a?->b();
// --------------- chain 1
//           -------- chain 2
// If $a is null then chain 2 is not evaluated, method b() is
not called, $foo returns null

  $a?->b($c->d());
// --------------- chain 1
//           ------- chain 2
// If $a is null, then chain 1 is stopped, method b() is not
called, `$c->d()` is not evaluated
```

```
    $a->b($c?->d());
// --------------- chain 1
//          -------- chain 2
// If $c is null, then chain 2 halts, method d() is not
called,`$a->b()` is set to null
```

The following elements are considered part of the chain:

- Array access ([])

- Property access (->)

- Nullsafe property access (?->)

- Static property access (::)

- Method call (->)

- Nullsafe method call (?->)

- Static method call (::)

Because we can create chains on chains, these elements will initiate a new logic chain:

- Arguments in a function call

- The expression in [] of an array access

- The expression in {} when accessing properties (->{})

The Benefits

The benefits of using nullsafe operators and short circuiting can be seen in several ways:

1. Avoiding surprises

   ```
   $pants = null;
   $pants?->dogs(getMeasurements());
   ```

55

Calling getMeasurements() is not desirable if $pants is null, as its result will be put to waste while possibly setting off other systems and methods, leading to unintended consequences. Let's say that while calling getMeasurements() we initialize several arrays or objects that are allocated to memory, reducing our computing resources. At the same time, this function builds out hundreds of lines of database (DB) information, say, prepping for an order of dog pants. This is a huge waste of resources and would not easily be caught by developers unless a critical eye looks at the size of the DB.

2. Clear optics of null returns

```
$pants = null;
$pants?->dog()->breed();
```

Without short circuiting, a check must be placed in every aspect of the chain to test where a null value is returned. Short circuiting allows us to easily see which property or method is causing the null value.

3. Mixing with other operators

```
$pants = null;
$poodlePants = $pants?->dog()['poodle'];
var_dump($poodlePants);

// Without short circuiting:
// Notice: Trying to access array offset on value of
type null
// NULL

// With short circuiting
// NULL
```

Because with short circuiting the array access ['poodle'] will be completely skipped, no notice is emitted.

Forbidden Uses

Writing

There were talks about using the nullsafe operator in the context of "writing," but due to technical difficulties this was left out of PHP 8. The following examples are not allowed.

```
$pants?->dog->breed = 'poodle';
// Can't use nullsafe operator in write context

foreach ([1, 2, 3] as $pants?->dog->breed) {}
// Can't use nullsafe operator in write context

unset($pants?->dog->breed);
// Can't use nullsafe operator in write context

[$pants?->dog->breed] = 'poodle';
// Assignments can only happen to writable values
```

References

Assigning the reference in a nullsafe chain is not allowed. References require l-values (memory locations like variables or properties), with nullsafe operators being capable of returning r-values (such as null). This is just not possible.

```
// 1
$x = &$pants?->dog;
// Compiler error: Cannot take reference of a nullsafe chain
```

```
// 2
takes_ref($pants?->dog);
// Error: Cannot pass parameter 1 by reference

// 3
function &return_by_ref($pants) {
    return $pants?->dpg;
    // Compiler error: Cannot take reference of a nullsafe chain
}
```

CHAPTER 6

Attributes V2

Date: 2020-03-09
Author: Benjamin Eberlei, Martin Schröder
Votes: 41 / 12

Months and months of back and forth have gone into this addition to PHP. The main sticking point was not whether or not it should be implemented, or how certain edge cases are not handled. The issue that sparked all of the debate is the user interface (UI); for example, the user experience of typing <<>> or @: (as the alternative method). Summarizing a majority of the conversation in the PHP mailing list is this quote from Mike Schinkel:

> *I am very excited to see this. I make heavy use of pseudo-attributes in both PhpDoc and using class constants, and having real attributes would be quite the boon.*
>
> *I do have a few concerns.*
>
> *1.   The syntax makes my eyes bleed.*

With that, let's dive into the RFC.

Attributes in PHP are defined by << >> or @: and can be applied to many elements of the language:

- Functions

- Classes, interfaces, and traits

- Class contents

- Class properties

- Class methods

- Function and method parameters

```
<<ExampleAttribute>>
class Pants
{
    <<ExampleAttribute>>
    public const PANTS = 'pants';

    <<ExampleAttribute>>
    public $pants;

    <<ExampleAttribute>>
    public function pants(<<ExampleAttribute>> $dog) { }
}
$object = new <<ExampleAttribute>> class () { };
<<ExampleAttribute>>
function pants1() { }
$pants2 = <<ExampleAttribute>> function () { };
$pants3 = <<ExampleAttribute>> fn () => 1;
```

Attributes are significantly better than docblock comments so that they warrant being introduced as a new language construct for several reasons:

- Namespacing prevents conflicts between different libraries using the same doc comment tag.

- Checking for attribute existence is a O(1) hash key test compared to unpredictable strstr performance or even parsing the docblock.

- Mapping attributes to classes ensures the attributes are correctly typed, reducing a major source of bugs in reliance on docblocks at runtime.

- There is visible demand for something like annotations based on their common use in so many different tools and communities. However, this will always be a confusing thing for newcomers to see in comments. In addition, the difference between /* and /** is still a very subtle source of bugs.

Although it might be possible to make PHP parse existing doc-comments and keep information as structured attributes, we would need to invoke an additional parser for each doc-comment. Doc-comments might not conform to context grammar and we have to decide what to do with grammar errors. Finally, this is another language inside PHP. This solution would be much more complex than introducing attributes and is not desired.

With attributes as proposed by this RFC, we reuse the existing syntax for expressions and constant expressions. The patch to the core for this functionality is small.

Attributes can be added before the declaration they are being attached to, similar to docblock comments. Attributes can also be added before or after a docblock comment. Each declaration (function, class, method, property, parameter, or class constant) could have one or more attributes. Each attribute might or might not have values attached to it, similar to a class constructor.

Because syntax is by far the most discussed point about this RFC, we also thought of an alternative by introducing a new token for attributes (T_ATTRIBUTE) defined as @: that the parser could look for.

```
@:WithoutArgument
@:SingleArgument(0)
@:FewArguments('Hello', 'World')
function foo() {}
```

Attribute Names Resolve to Classes

To namespace and avoid accidental reuse of attributes, during compilation the attribute names are resolved against all currently imported symbols.

```
use My\Attributes\thePants;
use My\Attributes\otherPants;

<<thePants("Hello")>>
<<Another\thePants("World")>>
<<\My\Attributes\otherPants("foo", "bar")>>
function foo() {}
```

Declaring an attribute class for this example looks like this:

```
namespace My\Attributes;
use PhpAttribute;
<<PhpAttribute>>
class thePants
{
    public $value;
    public function __construct(string $value)
    {
        $this->value = $value;
    }
}
```

The benefits of using attribute classes might feel like overkill, but they are tangible.

- Attributes can be converted by the Reflection API.

- Attribute verification via static analysis tools.

- Autocomplete support through IDEs.

Attribute Fetching

The Reflection API, mainly used in debugging, is used to retrieve attributes and store them for use. This does not execute or call constructors on any code unless an instance of the attribute is requested. Attributes are returned as strings of the attribute name and optional arguments if available. More information on the Reflection API and its uses can be found at `https://www.php.net/manual/en/book.reflection.php`.

Compiler and Userland Attributes

There are two different types of attributes that are used in PHP. Aptly named, compiler and userland attributes are used in their respective areas. The compiler attribute is an internal class used with `PhpCompilerAttribute` and userland attributes are used with `PhpAttribute`. Both of these are within the Zend bowels of PHP. If you have never ventured into the realm of php-src or Zend functions that is okay. The Zend functions and php-src are not commonplace, but are useful for debugging and applications such as xdebug.

Attribute Use Cases

The RFC gives some examples of possible use cases for attributes.

1. `<<jit>>`

    As we covered earlier, JIT comes with certain rules and settings. One such setting is the existing check for `@jit` in Opcache JIT that instructs the JIT to always optimize a function or method.

    PHP Core or extensions will want to check if certain declarations have an attribute or not.

One such example is the existing check for @jit in
Opcache JIT that instructs the JIT to always optimize
a function or method. An extension could be created
to take advantage of the built-in *op_array value
associated in the hashtables to check for the manual
declaration of JIT in an attribute.

```
static int zend_needs_manual_jit(const zend_op_array
*op_array)
    return op_array->attributes &&
        zend_hash_str_exists(op_array->attributes,
        "opcache\\jit", sizeof("opcache\\jit")-1));
}
```

Developers could then use an attribute instead of a
doc-comment:

```
use Opcache\Jit;
<<Jit>>
function foo() {}
```

2. Structured deprecation

Most languages that currently use attributes already
have the ability to deprecate classes, properties, or
constants within a code base. This could be useful
for maintainers of legacy or enterprise code.

```
// an idea, not part of the RFC
use Php\Attributes\Deprecated;
<<Deprecated("Use bar() instead")>>
function foo() {}
------ or
```

```
class Foo
{
    <<Deprecated()>>
    const BAR = 'BAR';
}
echo Foo::BAR;
// PHP Deprecated:  Constant Foo::BAR is
deprecated in test.php on line 7
```

3. Declaring event listener hooks on objects

   In Symfony, there is a method named
   EventSubscribers that requires users to declare
   which event is handled by which method on the
   class in the getSubscribedEvents() method. Users
   could refactor the code to use attributes to tag the
   methods instead.

```
// current code without attributes
class RequestSubscriber implements
EventSubscriberInterface
{
    public static function getSubscribedEvents(): array
    {
        return [RequestEvent::class =>
        'onKernelRequest'];
    }
    public function onKernelRequest(RequestEvent
    $event)
    {
    }
}
```

```php
// refactor to:
<<PhpAttribute>>
class Listener
{
    public $event;
    public function __construct(string $event)
    {
        $this->event = $event;
    }
}

class RequestSubscriber
{
    <<Listener(RequestEvent::class)>>
    public function onKernelRequest(RequestEvent
    $event)
    {
    }
}

// and the EventDispatcher to register
listeners based on attributes:

class EventDispatcher
{
    private $listeners = [];
    public function addSubscriber(object
    $subscriber)
    {
        $reflection = new
        ReflectionObject($subscriber);
```

```
foreach ($reflection->getMethods() as
$method) {
    // Does this method has Listener
    attributes?
    $attributes = $method->getAttribute
    s(Listener::class);

    foreach ($attributes as
    $listenerAttribute) {
        /** @var $listener Listener */
        $listener = $listenerAttribute-
        >newInstance();

        // with $listener instanceof
        Listener attribute,
        // register the method to the
        given Listener->event
        // as a callable
        $this->listeners[$listener-
        >event][] = [$subscriber,
        $method->getName()];
    }
}
}

public function dispatch($event, $args...)
{
    foreach ($this->listeners[$event] as
    $listener) {
        // invoke the listener callables
        registered to an event name
        $listener(...$args);
```

```
            }
        }
    }

    $dispatcher = new EventDispatcher();
    $dispatcher->addSubscriber(new
    RequestSubscriber());
    $dispatcher->dispatch(RequestEvent::class,
    $payload);
```

CHAPTER 7

Match Expression v2

Author: Ilija Tovilo

First there was "If ... then," then (no pun intended) there was "switch."
There was much rejoicing as switch gave developers a format in which
to offer a multitude of "if ... then" scenarios without the cumbersome
repetitive if ... then syntax. PHP 8 brings to us "Match," which
offers defined return values, no type coercion, no fallthrough, and
exhaustiveness.

```php
// PHP 7x
switch ($this->pants->mine['type']) {
    case pants::T_SELECT:
        $result = $this->SelectPants();
        break;
    case Pants::T_UPDATE:
        $result = $this->UpdatePants();
        break;
    case pants::T_DELETE:
        $result = $this->DeletePants();
        break;
    default:
        $this->syntaxError('SELECT, UPDATE or DELETE');
        break;
}
```

© Gunnard Engebreth 2021
G. Engebreth, *PHP 8 Revealed*, https://doi.org/10.1007/978-1-4842-6818-6_7

```php
// After
$result = match ($this->pants>mine['type']) {
    Pants::T_SELECT => $this->SelectPants(),
    Pants::T_UPDATE => $this->UpdatePants(),
    Pants::T_DELETE => $this->DeletePants(),
    default => $this->syntaxError('SELECT, UPDATE or DELETE'),
};
```

Return Values

Switch vs. Match

```php
switch (1) {
    case 0:
        $result = 'Pants';
        break;
    case 1:
        $result = 'Pants2';
        break;
    case 2:
        $result = 'Pants3';
        break;
}
echo $result;
//> Pants2
```

You can see how match makes this clear and simple.

```php
echo match (1) {
    0 => 'Pants',
    1 => 'Pants2',
    2 => 'Pants3',
};
//> Pants2
```

70

No Type Coercion

PHP uses nonstrict (==) comparisons when evaluating values in a switch statement. This can lead to unexpected (to some) results.

```
switch ('Pants') {
    case 0:
      $result = "Not Pants!\n";
      break;
    case 'Pants':
      $result = "This is Pants!\n";
      break;
}
echo $result;
//> Not Pants!
```

Match uses strict comparisons (===) instead. This happens regardless of the use of strict_types.

```
echo match ('Pants') {
    0 => "Not Pants!\n",
    'Pants' => "This is Pants!\n",
};
//> This is Pants!
```

No Fallthrough

One failure of switch in any language is the necessity to "break" out of the statement; otherwise, the execution will continue until the end. Match has an implied break after every line allowing for more streamlined code.

71

```
match ($anyKeypress) {
    Key::RETURN_ => saveIt(),
    Key::DELETE => deleteIt(),
};
```

Conditions can be chained together using commas.

```
echo match ($pants) {
    1, 2 => 'Pants 1 or 2',
    3, 4 => 'Pants 3 or 4',
};
```

Exhaustiveness

Another source of bugs in using the switch statement is not accounting for every possible case one might encounter. Match will throw an UnhandledMatchError, allowing for the error to be caught earlier.

```
$result = match ($option) {
    BinaryOperator::ADD => $lhs + $rhs,
};

// Throws when $option is BinaryOperator::SUBTRACT
```

CHAPTER 8

Mixed Type v2

Version: 0.9
Date: 2020-03-23
Author: Máté Kocsis, Danack
Implementation: https://github.com/php/php-src/pull/5313
Vote: 50 / 11

PHP 7 gave us scalar types, 7.1 brought nullables, objects were introduced in 7.2, and now union types have arrived in 8. Type information for most function parameters, function returns, and class properties can be declared, but there is still the need for a mixed type. Historically, PHP has allowed for type information to be unspecified, which, in the era of hyperspecification in programming, presents itself as an opportunity for clarity as mixed types.

The mixed type has a more specific purpose than its name suggests. It is meant to add types to parameters, class properties, and function returns to acknowledge that the type information wasn't forgotten about but this information could not be clarified further. This can also show that the programmer just decided not to do so. The mixed type would present itself as (array|bool|callable|int|float|null|object|resource|string).

Interestingly enough, examples of mixed type usage can be seen in PHP's own documentation as a pseudo-type.

```
var_dump ( mixed $expression [, mixed $... ] ) : void
```

G. Engebreth, *PHP 8 Revealed*, https://doi.org/10.1007/978-1-4842-6818-6_8

These comments are from the internals:

I ... cannot actually envision what code would actually accept that mess. :-)

—*Larry Garfield*

`var_dump()` *would be one example. Also caches that can store any userland value would be another reasonably common use.*

The general pattern is when you're handling someone else's "data" and have no restrictions on what type that data should be. That's actually the use-case that prompted me to help draft this RFC.

—*Dan Ack*

Now that we have Union types what places are there where the currently available type declarations are insufficient?

—*Larry Garfield*

A type that explicitly allows any type is more forwards compatible than writing out a union type. Compare this:

```
var_dump( mixed $expression [, mixed $... ] ) : void
```

to:

```
var_dump( null|bool|int|float|string|array|object|resource
$expression [, null|bool|int|float|string|array|object|reso
urce $... ] ) : void
```

If/when we add an "enum" type that is not a child type of any of the current types, the signature of that function doesn't need to change if it uses mixed, rather than the written out union type. Also, the "fitting on a line" problem.

—*Dan Ack*

Subclasses can widen a parameter type from a specific value type to mixed type. The reverse from mixed to specific is invalid per the LSP.

```
// Valid example
class A
{
    public function pants(int $value) {}
}
class B extends A
{
    // Parameter type widened from int to mixed is allowed
    public function pants(mixed $value) {}
}

// Invalid example
class A
{
    public function pants(mixed $value) {}
}
class B extends A
{
    // Parameter type narrowed from mixed to int
    // Fatal error
    public function pants(int $value) {}
}
```

Mixed return types could be narrowed in a subclass.

```
// Valid example
 class A
{
    public function foo(): mixed {}
}
```

```
class B extends A
{
    // return type from mixed to int is allowed
    public function pants(): int {}
}
```

Specific return type may not be widened using mixed.

```
// Invalid example
class C
{
    public function pants(): int {}
}
class D extends C
{
    // return type cannot be widened from int to mixed
    // Fatal error thrown
    public function pants(): mixed {}
}
```

Property types are invariant.

```
// Invalid example
class A
{
    public mixed $foo;
    public int $bar;
    public $baz;
}

class B extends A
{
    // property type cannot be narrowed from mixed to int
    // Fatal error thrown
```

```
    public int $foo;
}

class C extends A
{
    // property type cannot be widened from int to mixed
    // Fatal error thrown
    public mixed $bar;
}

class D extends A
{
    // property type cannot be added
    // Fatal error thrown
    public mixed $baz;
}

class E extends A
{
    // property type cannot be removed
    // Fatal error thrown
    public $foo;
}
```

CHAPTER 9

Weak Maps

Date: 2019-11-04
Author: Nikita Popov
Votes: 25 / 0

Weak Maps are more than what the kids use to describe MapQuest. They have to deal with garbage collecting and memory management. Let's first look at what a weak reference is. Weak References are used to reference an object while being eligible for garbage collection. Garbage collection occurs on objects that have no more references pointing to them. Weak Maps are collections of Weak References that do not prevent garbage collection on an object and will also be freed once the object is removed. There is already `SplObjectStorage` that allows for creating a map from objects to arbitrary values, but this is not the same as Weak Maps. More on this later. Now, I have scoured the Internet for examples (and there are several) of situations that would truly call for this. These situations are definitely one-offs. This is a feature that is most likely not going to be used by a majority of developers, but knowing your options will make you a top-tier coder.

So, how is this not like `SplObjectStorage`? I'm glad you asked. Popov pointed out multiple reasons in the RFC. First, the `spl_object_id()` values do not go away and are reused after the object is destroyed. Multiple objects can have the same object ID at different times. Second, there is no backward identification from object ID to object, thus preventing iteration over the map. Finally, destroying the object does not release the stored value under the ID.

© Gunnard Engebreth 2021
G. Engebreth, *PHP 8 Revealed*, https://doi.org/10.1007/978-1-4842-6818-6_9

Weak References were introduced in PHP 7.4 and are similar, but have several differences compared to PHP 8's Weak Map. Weak Map can be cloned, whereas Weak References cannot because the objects are unique. TypeError exceptions occur in Weak Maps when using a nonobject key $map[$key] or an offset*() method. Similarly, using $map[] to append to a Weak Map or reading a nonexistent key results in an Error exception. By-reference iteration of Weak Maps is supported as well. Weak References and Weak Map are similar in the fact that they are both not serializable and setting dynamic properties on them is forbidden. Popov touched on the serialization (or lack thereof).

> *Could you provide some context on why you think serialization support for WeakMap is important? As weak maps are essentially caching structures, serializing them doesn't seem particularly useful in the first place, but when combined with the quite unintuitive behavior the serialization would have, I feel that it is better to leave this to the user (same as WeakReference).*

> *Specifically what I mean by uninituitive is this: When you do a $s = serialize($weakMap), you'll get back a large payload string, but when you then try to do an unserialize($s) you'll get back an empty WeakMap (or worse: a weak map that will only become empty on the next GC), because all of those objects will get removed as soon as unserialization is finalized. That "works," but doesn't seem terribly useful and is likely doing to be a wtf moment.*

> —*Nikita Popov*

This is what a WeakMap class would look like.

```
$map = new WeakMap;
$obj = new stdClass;
$map[$obj] = 311;
var_dump($map);
```

```
// object(WeakMap)#1 (1) {
//   [0]=>
//   array(2) {
//     ["key"]=>
//     object(stdClass)#2 (0) {
//     }
//     ["value"]=>
//     int(311)
//   }
// }

// The key is removed from the map once the object is deleted.
unset($obj);
var_dump($map);
// object(WeakMap)#1 (0) {
// }
```

CHAPTER 10

New str_begins_ with() and str_ends_ with()

Date: 2020-03-25 (Updated: 2020-05-05)

Author: Will Hudgins

Votes: 51 / 4

Writing built-in functions for something that can be done with trivial one-liners isn't something we typically do.

—*Rasmus Lerdorf (2008)*

Twelve years later, these two functions have found a home in PHP 8. They are pretty straightforward, but their path to get here was not. The main issue was the fact that other already "free" functions in PHP could be used to determine the same solution. The other sticking point was whether or not to consider case sensitivity. This ultimately led to the functions being strictly case-sensative, the same as `str_contains()`. Also like `str_contains()` a space or " " is considered to be included in the string, therefore, always returning `true`.

```
str_starts_with ( string $haystack , string $needle ) : bool
str_ends_with ( string $haystack , string $needle ) : bool
```

CHAPTER 11

Str_contains

Date: 2020-02-17
Author: Philipp Tanlak
Votes: 43 / 9

I would like to know how many of you reading this currently have a makeshift function in their code base with a similar name and function. While researching this book I informed a colleague of this functionality and he proceeded to show me a `str_contains`" function in the very code base I use on a daily basis! Needless to say, this has been needed in PHP for a while. As the name implies, this function returns `true`/`false` if a string is contained in another given string. As per many other PHP functions, this is in (`$haystack, $needle`) form.

```php
<?php

str_contains("hive", "v"); // true
str_contains("brodels", "z"); // false

// using an empty string as $needle
str_contains("hive", ""); // true
str_contains("", "");      // true
```

Even though there were nine "no" votes on this, the discussion on the internals mailing list is very minimal and mostly positive.

© Gunnard Engebreth 2021
G. Engebreth, *PHP 8 Revealed*, https://doi.org/10.1007/978-1-4842-6818-6_11

CHAPTER 12

Bug Fixes

Stricter Type Checks for Arithmetic/Bitwise Operators

Date: 2020-04-02

Author: Nikita Popov

Votes: 57 / 0

This addition seems very straightforward. Currently, PHP evaluates this code with no problem:

```
var_dump([] % [311]);
// int(0)
```

PHP 8 will throw a type error whenever an arithmetic or bitwise operator is applied to an array, resource, or (nonoverloaded) object. The new behavior for all the arithmetic or bitwise operators (+, -, *, /, **, %, <<, >>, &, |, ^, ~, ++, --) when being applied in such a way will result in a TypeError thrown. The only exception is the use of addition with two array operands. This will remain legal. This will leave the other operands (null, bool, int, float, and string) with the same behavior as before.

© Gunnard Engebreth 2021
G. Engebreth, *PHP 8 Revealed*, https://doi.org/10.1007/978-1-4842-6818-6_12

Change Default PDO Error Mode

Version: 1.0
Date: 2020-03-28
Author: AllenJB
Votes: 49 / 2

By default, PHP does not report on PHP Data Objects (PDO) errors. This leaves many developers in the dark unless they know how to explicitly handle the reporting of these errors. `PDO::ERRMODE_EXCEPTION` will produce meaningful errors for developers without having to manage this on their own.

Treat Namespaced Names as Single Token

Date: 2020-06-15
Author: Nikita Popov
Votes: 38 / 4

Currently, namespaced names such as `Foo\Bar` are treated as a sequence of identifiers and namespace separator tokens.

```
Foo\Bar;
// T_STRING T_NS_SEPARATOR T_STRING
```

PHP 8 will consider these names as a single token. The main motivation behind this change is a developer's experience with their library using a reserved namespace name. The proposed solution will ensure that future developers will not have the same struggle with using reserved words in namespace names.

PHP acknowledges four kinds of namespaced names:

- Unqualified names like Pants, which coincide with identifiers.

- Qualified names like Pants\Dog.

- Fully qualified names like \Pants.

- Namespace-relative names like namespace\Pants.

Each of these kinds will be represented by a distinct token.

```
Pants;
// Before: T_STRING
// After:  T_STRING
// Rule:   {LABEL}

Pants\Dog;
// Before: T_STRING T_NS_SEPARATOR T_STRING
// After:  T_NAME_QUALIFIED
// Rule:   {LABEL}("\\"{LABEL})+

\Pants;
// Before: T_NS_SEPARATOR T_STRING
// After:  T_NAME_FULLY_QUALIFIED
// Rule:   ("\\"{LABEL})+

namespace\Pants;
// Before: T_NAMESPACE T_NS_SEPARATOR T_STRING
// After:  T_NAME_RELATIVE
// Rule:   "namespace"("\\"{LABEL})+
```

Saner String to Number Comparisons

Date: 2019-02-26

Author: Nikita Popov

Votes: 44 / 1

The state of string to number comparisons in PHP is "working" at best. There are many inconsistencies, `0 == "foobar"` being one of them. PHP 8 will make nonstrict comparisons more useful and less error prone by using multiple methods of comparison only if the string is actually numeric. If the string is not numeric, the number will be converted to a string and a string comparison will be performed.

PHP supports two different types of comparison operators: the strict comparisons `===` and `!==`, and the nonstrict comparisons `==`, `!=`, `>`, `>=`, `<`, `<=`, and `<=>`. The primary difference between them is that strict comparisons require both operands to be of the same type, and do not perform implicit type coercions.

Here is a before and after of nonstrict comparisons in PHP 8.

```
Comparison     | Before | After
-----------------------------
 0 == "0"      | true   | true
 0 == "0.0"    | true   | true
 0 == "foo"    | true   | false
 0 == ""       | true   | false
42 == "   42"  | true   | true
42 == "42foo"  | true   | false
```

Ensure Correct Signatures of Magic Methods

Version: 1.0
Date: 2020-04-05
Author: Gabriel Caruso
Implementation: https://github.com/php/php-src/pull/4177
Votes: 45 / 2

Currently magic methods such as __clone() and __isset() can have their signatures set to inappropriate values such as __clone(): float and __isset(): closure. This fix will add parameter and return type checks to promote proper usage of magic methods.

```
Foo::__call(string $name, array $arguments): mixed;
Foo::__callStatic(string $name, array $arguments): mixed;
Foo::__clone(): void;
Foo::__debugInfo(): ?array;
Foo::__get(string $name): mixed;
Foo::__invoke(mixed $arguments): mixed;
Foo::__isset(string $name): bool;
Foo::__serialize(): array;
Foo::__set(string $name, mixed $value): void;
Foo::__set_state(array $properties): object;
Foo::__sleep(): array;
Foo::__unserialize(array $data): void;
Foo::__unset(string $name): void;
Foo::__wakeup(): void;
```

Allow Trailing Comma in Closure Use Lists

Version: 0.2

Date: 2020-07-01

Author: Tyson Andre

Implementation: https://github.com/php/php-src/pull/5793

Votes: 49 / 0

Already accepted in argument and parameter lists, PHP 8 is catching use lists up with the rest of the code. In this example we will see how this is implemented.

```php
$longPants_longPantsVars = function (
    $longPant,
    $longerPant,
    $reallyLongPant,  // Trailing commas were allowed in
    parameter lists in PHP 8.0
) use (
    $longPant1,
    $longerPant2,
    $muchLongerPant3
) {
    // body
};
$longPants_LongPantVars(
    $longPantValue,
    $obj->longPantsMethod(),
    $obj->longPantsValue ?? $longDefault,
);
```

Remove Inappropriate Inheritance Signature Checks on Private Methods

Version: 0.3

Date: 2020-04-16

Author: Pedro Magalhães

Votes: 24 / 11

Per PHP object-oriented pogramming inheritance documentation, only public and protected methods are inherited. This is not a hard-and-fast rule, though. The rules seem to fall apart when you have a child method that is named the same as its parent final private, static private, or concrete private method.

```php
<?php
class A
{
    final private function finalPrivate() {
        echo __METHOD__ . PHP_EOL;
    }
}

class B extends A
{
    private function finalPrivate() {
        echo __METHOD__ . PHP_EOL;
    }
}
```

That code produces this result:

```
Fatal error: Cannot override final method A::finalPrivate()
```

PHP 8 will allow and handle code like this:

```php
<?php
class A
{
    function callYourPrivate() {
        $this->myPrivate();
    }

    function notOverriden_callYourPrivate() {
        $this->myPrivate();
    }
    final private function myPrivate() {
        echo __METHOD__ . PHP_EOL;
    }
}

class B extends A
{
    function callYourPrivate() {
        $this->myPrivate();
    }
    private function myPrivate() {
        echo __METHOD__ . PHP_EOL;
    }
}

$a = new A();
$a->callYourPrivate();
$a->notOverriden_callYourPrivate();

$b = new B();
$b->callYourPrivate();
$b->notOverriden_callYourPrivate();
```

Here are the results:

```
Warning: Private methods cannot be final as they are never
overridden by other classes in ...
A::myPrivate
A::myPrivate
B::myPrivate
A::myPrivate
```

Saner Numeric Strings

Version: 1.4
Date: 2020-06-28
Original Author: Andrea Faulds
Original RFC: PHP RFC: Permit trailing whitespace in numeric strings
Author: George Peter Banyard
Implementation: https://github.com/php/php-src/pull/5762

PHP includes the concept of a numeric string, or a string that can be interpreted as a numeric. The numeric-ness of a string can be described in four ways: *numeric, leading-numeric, non-numeric,* or *integer.*

- A *numeric string* is a string containing numbers, with optional whitespace at the beginning: "311" or " 311"

- A *leading-numeric string* is a string containing numbers with non-numeric characters (whitespace included) at the end: "311abc" or "311 "

- A *non-numeric string* is neither a numeric string or a non-numeric string.

- An *integer* string is a numeric string used as an array index, but it has additional constraints of foregoing leading non-numeric or whitespace characters: "311"

Arithmetic or bitwise operators will perform a conversion of all operands to their numeric or integer equivalent while also logging a notice or warning when the string is malformed or invalid. The exception to this is the &, |, and ^ bitwise operators when the operands are both strings and the ~ operator is used, in which case it will perform the operation on the ASCII values that make up the strings and the result will also be a string.

The Problem

Numerical strings currently behave as follows:

- Numeric strings with leading whitespaces are perceived as "more numeric" than numeric strings with trailing whitespaces.

- Strings such as UUIDs like ("fe3d2fee-575d-4122-b75b-11dc068027fd") could be falsely interpreted as numbers, leading to unpredictable results.

- \is_numeric() and weak-mode parameter checks will return inconsistent results.

- Unintuitive and inconsistent behavior results from leading-numeric strings.

Proposal

The unification of the various numeric string modes into a single concept of numeric characters only when both leading and trailing whitespace is allowed is the proposed solution, declaring any other type of string as non-numeric and throwing TypeErrors when attempting to be used in a numeric context. This will change E_NOTICE "A non well formed numeric value encountered" to E_WARNING "A non-numeric value encountered" with the caveat being if the leading-numeric string contained only trailing whitespace.

Type Declarations

```
function pants(int $i) { var_dump($i); }
pants("123   "); // int(123)
pants("123abc"); // TypeError
```

\is_numeric returns true for numeric strings with any trailing whitespace.

```
var_dump(is_numeric("311   ")); // bool(true)
```

String Offsets

```
$str = 'The Pants;
var_dump($str['5str']);    // string(1) "a" with E_WARNING
                           //     "Illegal string offset '5str'"
var_dump($str['5.4']);     // string(1) "a" with E_WARNING
                           //     "String offset cast occurred"
var_dump($str['promises']); // TypeError
```

Arithmetic Operations

```
var_dump(311 + "311   "); // int(622)
var_dump(311 + "311abc"); // int(622) with E_WARNING
                          //     "A non-numeric value encountered"
var_dump(311 + "string"); // TypeError
```

Using the ++ and -- operators will convert numeric strings with trailing whitespace to integers or floats, as appropriate, instead of applying the alphanumeric increment rules:

```
$c = "4 ";
var_dump(++$c); // int(5)
```

String-to-String Comparisons

```
var_dump("311" == "311   "); // bool(true)
```

Bitwise Operations

```
var_dump(311 & "311   ");   // int(311)
var_dump(311 & "311abc"); // int(311) with E_WARNING
                             "A non-numeric value encountered"
var_dump(311 & "abc");     // TypeError
```

Make Sorting Stable

Date: 2020-05-12
Author: Nikita Popov
Votes: 45 / 0
Implementation: https://github.com/php/php-src/pull/5236

Stability in PHP sorts has been an issue for some time. PHP 5 initially offered unstable sorting, with PHP 7 resolving this for arrays of 16 elements or less. PHP 8 now offers stable sorting once and for all. The issue at hand is that if multiple elements in the input array compare equal, the sorting takes place adjacently. If the sort is found to be unstable, the relative order of the elements is not guaranteed, therefore appearing random. Stabilizing the sort will guarantee that elements that are equal will retain the order initially assigned in the original array. This includes sort, rsort, usort, asort, arsort, uasort, ksort, krsort, uksort, and array_multisort, as well as corresponding methods on ArrayObject.

Let's take a look at what unstable sorting looks like.

```
$array = [
    'cat' => 1,
    'dog' => 1,
```

```
    'apple' => 0,
    'banana' => 0,
];
asort($array);
```

This is the result of that unstable sorting:

```
['banana' => 0, 'apple' => 0, 'cat' => 1, 'dog' => 1]
['apple' => 0, 'banana' => 0, 'dog' => 1, 'cat' => 1]
['banana' => 0, 'apple' => 0, 'dog' => 1, 'cat' => 1]
```

A stable sort would consistently return this:

```
['apple' => 0, 'banana' => 0, 'cat' => 1, 'dog' => 1]
```

Stable sorting is accomplished now by explicitly storing the original order of elements, but it is highly inefficient and hacky. To achieve the new stable sort, the current zend_sort will be used with an additional effort to store the original order of the array elements that will be used as a fallback if the use case is needed.

Stable sorting also comes with a change in how comparison functions behave. Per the documentation, a comparison function must return an integer smaller than, equal to, or greater than zero. This is fine; however, because of the nature of PHP, a boolean is also possible to be returned whether a value is greater. This is fixed in PHP 8 in two ways. First, there will be a warning thrown noting the deprecation, once per sort.

```
usort(): Returning bool from comparison function is deprecated,
return an integer less than, equal to, or greater than zero
```

The second piece is that if a boolean is returned and is false, the comparison will happen again, this time swapping the arguments allowing for PHP to determine if the false was actually "equal" or "smaller than." This behavior is planned for removal in future versions of PHP.

CHAPTER 13

Miscellaneous Additions

Class Constructor Property Promotion

In previous versions of PHP, the declarations needed to define a simple value object were tedious and repetitive.

```php
class Pants {
    public float $x;
    public float $y;
    public float $z;

    public function __construct(
        float $x = 0.0,
        float $y = 0.0,
        float $z = 0.0,
    ) {
        $this->x = $x;
        $this->y = $y;
        $this->z = $z;
    }
}
```

© Gunnard Engebreth 2021
G. Engebreth, *PHP 8 Revealed*, https://doi.org/10.1007/978-1-4842-6818-6_13

In this new feature, PHP offers a more optimized method for achieving a new class.

```php
class Pants {
    public function __construct(
        public float $x = 0.0,
        public float $y = 0.0,
        public float $z = 0.0,
    ) {}
}
```

Constraints

Nonabstract constructors are not allowed and will result in errors.

```php
// Error: Not a constructor.
function pants(private $x) {}

abstract class Pants {
    // Error: Abstract constructor.
    abstract public function __construct(private $x);
}

interface Pants {
    // Error: Abstract constructor.
    public function __construct(private $x);
}
```

If one were to use traits, class constructor property promotion would be allowed. Promoted properties must also use one of the visibility keywords (public, private, protected). The use of var is not supported.

```php
class Pants {
    // Error: "var" keyword is not supported.
    public function __construct(var $foo) {}
}
```

The same restrictions as normal property declarations apply to properties declared through promoted parameters. This means that declaring the same property twice is not possible.

```
class Test {
    public $prop;

    // Error: Redeclaration of property.
    public function __construct(public $prop) {}
}
```

Callable types are not usable because they are not supported as a property type.

```
class Test {
    // Error: Callable type not supported for properties.
    public function __construct(public callable $callback) {}
}
```

New fdiv() Function

The fdiv() function will perform a floating-point division while treating division by zero as a perfectly legal operation, and will not emit any kind of diagnostic in that case. Instead it will return the INF/-INF/NAN result mandated by IEEE-754. It mirrors the existing fmod() function.

—Nikita Popov

Currently division by zero results in unpredictable behavior. Per the new engine warnings in PHP 8, Popov wanted to add fdiv() to the fmod() and intdiv() family.

Let's look at some examples of this behavior.

```
$output = intdiv(1, 0);
Fatal error: Uncaught DivisionByZeroError:
$output = 1 % 0;
Fatal error: Uncaught DivisionByZeroError
----
actually dividing by zero does not behave the same.
$output = 1 / 0;
Warning: Division by zero.
```

fdiv will follow IEEE-754 semantics and return INF/-INF/NaN without throwing a critical error.

Always Generate Fatal Error for Incompatible Method Signatures

Date: 2019-04-08

Author: Nikita Popov

Vote: 39 / 3

This is yet another error escalation. Incompatible method signatures will always throw a fatal error. Previous versions would throw warnings or fatal errors, but PHP 8 brings all errors together as fatal.

Arrays Starting with a Negative Index

Version: 0.4

Date: 2017-04-20

Author: Pedro Magalhães

Vote: 17 / 2

Any given array that has a number n for the first numeric key will be implicitly assigned the next key as either n+1 (if n >= 0) or 0 (if n < 0). PHP 8 will not handle this differently, by always assigning the next key as n+1 regardless of the value of the first key.

Implement New DOM Living Standard APIs in ext/dom

Version: 0.3

Date: 2019-09-15

Author: Benjamin Eberlei (beberlei@php.net), Thomas Weinert

Vote: 37 / 0

The original Document Object Model or DOM, created to be the interface for HTML and XML, was established by the W3 in 2004 but has been taken over by the Web Hypertext Application Technology Working Group (WHATWG) and transformed into the Living Standard. This standard has been adopted because the new API improves the traversal and manipulation of the data. This adoption also ensures that as the standard evolves, so does PHP support. There are a few deviations from the standard itself mainly because it is written for the browser or JavaScript and PHP must adapt to make these situations work.

Implement

```php
<?php
interface DOMParentNode
{
    /** access to the first child of this node that is a
    DOMElement */
    public readonly ?DOMElement $firstElementChild;
```

```
    /** access to the last child of this node that is a
    DOMElement */
    public readonly ?DOMElement $lastElementChild;

    /** counts all child nodes that are DOMElements */
    public readonly int $childElementCount;

    /** appends one or many nodes to the list of children
    behind the last child node */
    public function append(...DOMNode|string|null $nodes) : void;

    /** prepends one or many nodes to the list of children
    before the first child node */
    public function prepend(...DOMNode|string|null $nodes) : void;
}

class DOMDocument implements DOMParentNode {}
class DOMElement implements DOMParentNode {}
class DOMDocumentFragment implements DOMParentNode {}

interface DOMChildNode
{
    /** Returns the previous node in the same hierarchy that is
    a DOMElement or NULL if there is none */
    public readonly ?DOMElement $previousElementSibling;

    /** Returns the next node in the same hierachy that is a
    DOMElement or NULL if there is none */
    public readonly ?DOMElement $nextElementSibling;

    /** acts as a simpler version of $element->parentNode->
    removeChild($element); */
    public function remove() : void;

    /** add passed node(s) before the current node */
    public function before(...DOMNode|string|null $nodes) : void;
```

```
/** add passed node(s) after the current node */
public function after(...DOMNode|string|null $nodes) : void;

/** replace current node with new node(s), a combination of
remove() + append() */
public function replaceWith(...DOMNode|string|null $nodes) :
void;
}
class DOMElement implements DOMChildNode {}
class DOMCharacterData implements DOMChildNode {}
```

The living standard contains an intermediate trait (interface) DOMNonDocumentTypeChildNode that defines the previousElementSibling and nextElementSibling properties. PHP does not allow interfaces to declare properties; therefore, this interface is not available for use but the properties are available on each class implementing DOMChildNode. Two other methods, querySelector and querySelectorAll, are also left out of this implantation. These are geared toward Cascading Style Sheets (CSS) selecting and there are already specific libraries (PhpCss or Symfony CSS Selector) that can handle this functionality much better.

Static Return Type

Date: 2020-01-08

Author: Nikita Popov

Implementation: https://github.com/php/php-src/pull/5062

Vote: 54 / 0

Currently, using the static special class name will refer to the actual class on which a method was called. This applies whether the method is inherited or not. This is referred to as *late static binding* (LSB). LSB works by storing the class named in the last nonforwarding call. For static method calls, this is the class explicitly named (to the left of the :: operator usually); in the case of nonstatic method calls, it is the class of the object.

A forwarding call is a static one that is introduced by self::, parent::, or static::, and also, if going up in the class hierarchy, forward_static_ call().

```
class A {
    public function test(): self {}
}
class B extends A {
    public function test(): static {}
}
class C extends B {}
class A {
    public function test(): A {}
}
class B extends A {}
class C extends B {
    public function test(): static {}
}
```

Variable Syntax Tweaks

This is for updates to the Uniform Variable Syntax RFC in PHP 7.

Date: 2020-01-07

Author: Nikita Popov

Implementation: https://github.com/php/php-src/pull/5061

Vote: 47 / 0

There are four main types of "dereferencing" operations in PHP:

- Array: $foo[$bar], $foo{$bar}

- Object: $foo->bar, $foo->bar()

- Static: Foo::$bar, Foo::bar(), Foo::BAR

- Call: foo()

Interpolated and Noninterpolated Strings

Currently, noninterpolated strings like "pants" are considered fully dereferenceable; that is, constructions such as "pants"[0] or "pants"-> shorts() are considered syntactically legal. Interpolated strings such as "pants$shorts" are nondereferenceable.

Magic, Class, and Regular Constants

Magic constants such as __PANTS__ will now be treated like normal constants and allowed to be array-dereferenceable.

PANTS[0] and __PANTS__[0]

Class constants, similarly, are dereferenceable using the PANTS{0} and PANTS->length().

Class Constant Dereferenceability

Currently Foo::$bar::$baz is legal, whereas Foo::BAR::$baz is not. PHP 8 will change this so that Foo::BAR::$baz and Foo::BAR::BAZ become legal.

Arbitrary Expression Support for new and instanceof

PHP 8 also will introduce the syntax new (expr) and $x instanceof (expr).

Add Stringable Interface

Version: 0.9

Date: 2020-01-15

Author: Nicolas Grekas

Vote: 29 / 9

The stringable interface will add a stringable interface to all classes that implement the __toString() method. There are two purposes of this interface. The first is to allow use of string|Stringable to express string|object-with-__toString(). The second is to provide a forward upgrade path from PHP 7 to PHP 8.

get_debug_type

Date: 2020-02-15

Author: Mark Randall

Vote: 42 / 3

This addition to PHP 8 differs from the obvious sibling get_type() by returning the native type name int instead of integer while also resolving class names. The main purpose of this function is to replace a more complicated process when dealing with types that cannot be handled by PHP at runtime by existing checking based on parameter types. Specifically this is beneficial when dealing with parameter types in arrays.

```
$pants = $arr['key'];
if (!($pants instanceof Hive)) {
    throw new TypeError('Expected ' . Hive::class . ' got ' .
    (is_object($pants) ? get_class($pants) : gettype($pants)));
}
```

Table 13-1 lists the different return values for gettype and get_debug_type.

Table 13-1. *Return Values for gettype and get_debug_type*

Value	get_debug_type()	gettype()
0	int	integer
0.1	float	double
True	bool	boolean
False	bool	boolean
"hello"	string	
[]	array	
Null	null	NULL
A class with name "Pants\Hive"	Pants\Hive	object
An anonymous class	class@anonymous	object
A resource	resource (xxx)	resource
A closed resource	resource (closed)	

```
// PHP 8 would allow for
if (!($pants instanceof Hive)) {
  throw new TypeError('Expected ' . Hive::class . ' got ' .
  get_debug_type($pants));
}
$pants>someHiveMethod();
```

This was welcomed into PHP with little controversy. Popov gave a little more detail at the time of voting.

Given the naming discussion, I think there's one important part to highlight here: For anonymous classes, this returns just "class@anonymous"*, not* "class@anonymous\0SOME_RANDOM_UNIQUE_STRING_HERE"*. Thus this functionality certainly can't be under a* ::type *construct (which should return the full name), and even* get_canonical_type() *seems inappropriate.*

This function is specifically useful for including type names in error messages or similar, thus get_debug_type() *...*

—*Nikita Popov*

New preg_last_error_msg()

Author: Nico Oelgart

PHP has a standard class of functions known as Perl Compatable Regular Expressions (PCRE). PCRE functions allow for the standard use of regular expressions in PHP. In previous visions of PHP users were only given preg_last_error(), which returns error codes. With preg_last_error_msg() we can now change this:

```php
<?php
preg_match('/(?:\D+|<\d+>)*[!?]/', 'foobar foobar foobar');
var_dump(preg_last_error()); // 2
var_dump(preg_last_error_msg()); // Backtrack limit was
exhausted
```

Add CMS Support

Date: 2020-05-13
    Author: Eliot Lear

No, this does not have to do with WordPress, Laravel, Drupal, or the like! Cryptographic Message Syntax (CMS), is a newer version of PKCS#7. PKCS#7 (Public Key Cryptography Standards) developed by RSA Security, LLC, is the standard in which the generation and verification of digital signatures and cerificates is managed by a public key infrastructure (PKI). This is the encryption standard currently used in email as well as Internet of Things devices.

The relationship between the PKCS#7 and OpenSSL functions is shown in Table 13-2.

Table 13-2. *PKCS#7 and OpenSSL Functions*

PKCS#7 Function	New CMS Function
openssl_pkcs7_encrypt( )	openssl_cms_encrypt( )
openssl_pkcs7_decrypt( )	openssl_cms_decrypt( )
openssl_pkcs7_sign( )	openssl_cms_sign( )
openssl_pkcs7_verify ( )	openssl_cms_verify( )
openssl_pkcs7_read ( )	openssl_cms_read( )

```
function openssl_cms_sign(string $infile, string $outfile,
$signcert, $signkey, ?array $headers, int $flags = 0, int
$encoding = OPENSSL_ENCODING_SMIME, ?string $extracertsfilename
= null): bool {}
```

This function signs a file with an X.509 certificate and key. The arguments are as follows.

- $infile: The name of the file to be signed

- $outfile: The name of the file in which to deposit the results

- $signcert: The name of the file containing the signing certificate

- $signkey: The name of the file containing the key associated with $signcert

- $headers: An array of headers to be included in S/MIME output

- $flags: Flags to be passed to cms_sign()

- $encoding: The encoding of the output file

- $extracertsfilename: Intermediate certificates to be included in the signature

```
function openssl_cms_verify(string $filename, int $flags = 0,
string $signerscerts = UNKNOWN, array $cainfo = UNKNOWN, string
$extracerts = UNKNOWN, string $content = UNKNOWN, string $pk7
= UNKNOWN, string $sigfile = UNKNOWN, $encoding = OPENSSL_
ENCODING_SMIME ): bool {}
```

This function verifies a CMS signature, either attached or detached, with the specified encoding.

Here are the arguments:

- $filename: The input file

- $flags: Flags that would be passed to cms_verify

- $signercerts: A file for the signer certificate and optionally intermediate certificates

- $cainfo: An array containing self-signed certificate authority certificates

- $extracerts: A file containing additional intermediate certificates

- $content: A file pointing to the content when signatures are detached

- $pk7: A file to save the signature to

- $encoding: One of three supported encodings (PEM/DER/SMIME).

This returns TRUE on success and FALSE on failure.

```
function openssl_cms_encrypt(string $infile, string $outfile,
$recipcerts, ?array $headers, int $flags = 0, int $encoding =
OPENSSL_ENCODING_SMIME,  int $cipher = OPENSSL_CIPHER_RC2_40):
bool {}
```

This function encrypts content to one or more recipients, based on the certificates that are passed to it.

Here are the arguments:

- $infile: The file to be encrypted

- $outfile: The output file

- $recipcerts: Recipients to encrypt to

- $headers: Headers to include when S/MIME is used

- $flags: Flags to be passed to CMS_sign

- $encoding: An encoding to output

- $cipher: A cypher to use

This returns the value TRUE on success or FALSE on failure.

```
function openssl_cms_decrypt(string $infilename, string
$outfilename, $recipcert, $recipkey = UNKNOWN, int $encoding =
OPENSSL_ENCODING_SMIME): bool {}
```

This function decrypts a CMS message. Here are the arguments:

- `$infilename`: The name of a file containing encrypted content

- `$outfilename`: The name of the file in which to deposit the decrypted content

- `$recipcert`: The name of the file containing a certificate of the recipient

- `$recipkey`: The name of the file containing a PKCS#8 key

- `$encoding`: The encoding of the input file.

This function returns TRUE on success and FALSE on failure.

```
function openssl_cms_read(string $infilename, &$certs): bool {}
```

The function performs the exact analog to `openssl_pkcs7_read()`. New constants are also included.

```
OPENSSL_ENCODING_CMS /* encoding is a CMS-encoded message */
OPENSSL_ENCODING_DER /* encoding is DER (Distinguished Encoding
Rules) */
OPENSSL_ENCODING_PEM /* encoding is PEM (Privacy-Enhanced Mail) */
OPENSSL_CMS_DETACHED
OPENSSL_CMS_TEXT
OPENSSL_CMS_NOINTERN
OPENSSL_CMS_NOVERIFY
OPENSSL_CMS_NOCERTS
OPENSSL_CMS_NOATTR
OPENSSL_CMS_BINARY
OPENSSL_CMS_NOSIGS
```

Allow ::class on Objects

Date: 2020-01-09

Author: Nikita Popov

Vote: 60 / 0

In previous versions of PHP the constant ::class allows for the fully qualified class name to be accessed. This constant takes into consideration the use and current namespace available.

```
namespace 311\Albums;
use Grass\Roots;
use Roots\Music as Album;

class Pants {}
// `use` statement
echo Roots::class; // 'Grass\Roots"

// `use` X `as` Y
echo Album::class; // "Roots\Music"

// Current namespace
echo Albums::class; // "311\Albums\Pants"
```

Previous versions of PHP throw a fatal error when ::class is used on an object, but in PHP 8 this now performs as expected.

```
$object = new Grass\Roots;
echo $object::class;
// "Grass\Roots"
```

If $object is an object, then $object::class returns get_class($object). Otherwise it throws a TypeError exception.

```
$object = new stdClass;
var_dump($object::class); // "stdClass"
```

```
$object = null;
var_dump($object::class); // TypeError
```

Object-Based token_get_all() Alternative

Date: 2020-02-13

Author: Nikita Popov nikic@php.net

Implementation: https://github.com/php/php-src/pull/5176

Vote: 47 / 0

Popov proposed the PhpToken::getAll() method is the replacement for token_get_all(), which will return an array of PhpToken objects instead of a mix of strings and arrays. There are two main reasons for this. The first is that returning an array of objects will standardize the return structure. Now, developers only need to expect an array of objects instead of the possibilities of single-character strings or arrays. The second and most beneficial is a reduction of memory usage when using an array.

```
Default:
    Memory Usage: 14.0MiB
    Time: 0.43s (for 100 tokenizations)
TOKEN_AS_OBJECT:
    Memory Usage: 8.0MiB
    Time: 0.32s (for 100 tokenizations)
```

Additionally the method getTokenName() is included, which is mainly useful for debugging purposes. For single-char tokens with IDs below 256, it returns the extended ASCII character corresponding to the ID. For known tokens, it returns the same result as token_name(). For unknown tokens, it returns null.

Here is the new class implementation:

```php
class PhpToken {
    /** A T_* constant, or an integer < 256 representing a
    single-char token. */
    public int $id;
    /** The context of the token. */
    public string $text;
    /** starting line number (1-based) of the token. */
    public int $line;
    /** starting position (0-based) in the tokenized string. */
    public int $pos;
/**

    * Same as token_get_all(), but returning array of PhpToken.
    * @return static[]
    */
    public static function getAll(string $code, int $flags = 0):
    array;

    final public function __construct(int $id, string $text,
    int $line = -1, int $pos = -1);
    /** Get the name of the token. */
    public function getTokenName(): ?string;
```

Because the PhpToken::getAll() method returns static[], extending this class is easily done.

```php
class thePhpToken extends PhpToken {
    public function getLowerText() {
        return strtolower($this->text);
    }
}
```

```
$tokens = thePhpToken::getAll($code);
var_dump($tokens[0] instanceof thePhpToken); // true
$tokens[0]->getLowerText(); // works
```

Validation for Abstract Trait Methods

Date: 2020-02-07

Author: Nikita Popov

Implementation: https://github.com/php/php-src/pull/5068

Vote: 52 / 0

Traits in PHP are similar to classes but intended for reuse in multiple instances. For example:

```php
<?php
trait CustomReturn {
    function getFirstReturnType() { /*1*/ }
    function getFirstReturnDesc() { /*2*/ }
}

class thisFakeMethod extends FakeMethod {
    use CustomReturn;
    /* ... */
}

class thisFakeFunction extends FakeFunction {
    use CustomReturn;
    /* ... */
}
?>
```

PHP 8 will always validate the signature of abstract trait method against the implementing method *independent* of its origin. A fatal error is generated if the implementing method is not compatible with the abstract trait method. Noncompatibility is defined as follows:

- The signature must be compatible, which includes parity compatibility, contravariant parameter type compatibility, and covariant return type compatibility.

- The static-ness of the methods must match.

In addition, the ability for the declaration of abstract private methods in traits only is now available. Abstract private methods are a contradiction in terms, because the method declaring the implementation would not be visible from the class issuing the requirement. Traits, however, provide well-defined access to abstract private methods, because trait methods have access to private methods of the using class.

Throw Expression

Date: 2020-03-21
Author: Ilija Tovilo
Implementation: https://github.com/php/php-src/pull/5279
Vote: 46 / 3

Throw is used in conjunction with catch to deal with exceptions within programming logic. Surrounded by a try block, one can throw an exception to be caught and dealt with instead of breaking the code. Throw, however, has only been used in this type of scenario and is unavailable to be used as an expression. This would allow for use of throw with arrow functions, the coalesce operator, and the ternary/elvis operator.

```
$pants = fn() => throw new Exception();
$pants = $nullyMcNull ?? throw new NullException();
$pants = $isFalse ?: throw new FalseException();
```

```
$pants = !empty($array)
    ? reset($array)
    : throw new EmptyException();
$isWinning && throw new Exception();
$isWinning || throw new Exception();
$isWinning and throw new Exception();
$isWinning or throw new Exception();
```

Precedence will also become important. Everything after the `throw` statement will be considered with a higher importance. That being said, `throw` will take the lowest operator precedence. This makes sense because, in general, the `throw` should be at the end of your logic statement anyway.

```
throw (static::wrongPasswordException());
throw ($cheeseIsFree ? new payForCheeseException() : new
noCheeseException());
throw ($foreverAlone ?? new Exception());
throw ($lightning = new Exception());
throw ($promises ??= new words());
throw ($fu && $gazi ? new selling() : new buying());
```

The one place that specificity needs to be asserted is with short-circuit operators. Parentheses must be used to discern priority, if one chooses to do so.

```
$transistor || (throw new Exception('$transistor must be
resistor') && $unplugged || (throw new Exception('$unplugged
must be resistor')));
```

Locale-Independent Float to String Cast

Version: 1.0

Date: 2020-03-11

Author: George Peter Banyard, Máté Kocsis

Implementation: https://github.com/php/php-src/pull/5224

Vote: 42 / 1

Casting floats to strings in PHP has been an issue for a while. This issue occurs because different countries represent the decimal character (. or ,) differently. For example, 3.14 is fairly standard in the United States and can be identified as the beginning of the value of pi. If you were developing in Poland, however, you would be using "3,14". The main problem with this difference is when using a float to string cast, the results are inconsistent because of the locale. This addition would standardize these issues with "." as the dominant decimal placeholder.

```
setlocale(LC_ALL, "pl_PL");
$f = 3.11;
(string) $f;              // 3,11 would become 3.11
strval($f);               // 3,11 would become 3.11
print_r($f);              // 3,11 would become 3.11
var_dump($f);             // float(3,11) would become float(3.11)
debug_zval_dump($f);      // float(3,11) would become float(3.11)
settype($f, "string");    // 3,11 would become 3.11
implode([$f]);            // 3,11 would become 3.11
xmlrpc_encode($f);        // 3,11 would become 3.11
```

This behavior is not unprecedented in userland. The PDO extension, for example, takes advantage of this to standardize string representation of floats. Locale independence is also used in var_export, serialize, and json_encode. printf, however, already having an option to specify a nonlocale-aware conversion with %f, is left unchanged.

Noncapturing Catches

Version: 0.9
Date: 2020-04-05
Author: Max Semenik
Implementation: https://github.com/php/php-src/pull/5345
Vote: 48 / 1

Briefly, I want to be able to do the following:

```
try {
foo();
catch (SomeExceptionClass) {
bar();
}}
```

Please share your thoughts! :)

—Max Semenik

Looks good to me.

—Stas Malyshev

The try/catch paradigm in programming allows for one code block to be defined and tested for errors (try) while defining another code block to handle said error (catch). In PHP this functions with the use of a variable in the catch block that assigns itself to the error.

```
try {
    foo();
} catch (weekendException $ex) {
    die($ex->showMessage());
}
```

would turn into

```
try {
    foo();
} catch (weekendException) {
    echo "This does not work on the weekend";
}
```

This addition wil no longer require the specification of a variable. The intention of the catch is clear and therefore there is no need for any other specifics.

Always Available JSON Extension

Version: 0.3

Date: 2020-04-29

Author: Tyson Andre

Implementation: https://github.com/php/php-src/pull/5495

Votes: 56 / 0

Through this addition, the PHP team is taking the first step in moving JSON from a PECL extension to a core feature of PHP. Currently the only way to disable JSON in a PHP build is through ./configure --disable-json, which leaves open the possibility of code requiring JSON to malfunction. The only noted reason for disabling JSON in previous versions of PHP was due to licensing issues that have since been resolved.

This change would have backward compatibility issues, however. The use of --enable-json or --disable-json in scripts or command-line interface (CLI) instructions will need to be updated as these options will no longer exist. The same is for any code using extension_loaded('json'), as this will always be true.

zend.exception_string_param_max_len: Configurable String Length in getTraceAsString()

Since 2003, two very useful functions have been limited to 15 bytes of information. `Throwable->getTraceAsString()` and `Throwable->__toString()` are expected to return stack traces to developers eagerly waiting to squash bugs in their code. Until PHP 8, these have returned semiuseful strings like `"/path/to/the/vesion/file.php 1349 function(whe ..."`, which is realistically not enough information to be usable when considering the use of paths, URLs, and UUIDs.

The solution to this is an `.ini` setting, `zend.exception_string_param_max_len`, which would allow changing the byte limit of the string to any value from 0 to 1000000. The default value would be kept at 15 if no value was set. A concern with this, however, is that with the increase of exposed data, the risk of unintended sensitive data being made available also increases.

```
function badHTMLRenderingExample(string $secretCode, string
$secretPassword) {
    echo "<h1>Welcome AOL</h1>\n";
    try {
        process($secretCode);
    } catch (Exception $e) {
        // The output will include both $secretCode and
        $secretPassword.
        // in PHP 7x, only 15 bytes would be displayed.
        echo "ID: 10 T error, please feed the dev team: $e\n";
    }
}
```

The default setting of 15 bytes will keep legacy code that actually does this safe unless the `.ini` setting is changed.

Unbundle ext/xmlrpc

Version: 1.0
Date: 2020-05-12
Author: Christoph M. Becker
Unbundled via `https://github.com/php/php-src/pull/5640`
Votes: 50 / 0

> *There does not seem to be a strong need to signal that people should stop using it ASAP. The extension (and more importantly, the underlying library) has been unmaintained for many years already and the move to PECL will not change things materially in that regard.*
>
> —*Nikita Popov*

`ext/xmlrpc` is, currently, a necessary evil in PHP. XML-RPC, for those who do not know, is the specification that allows for the use of XML between systems, and hence is necessary. Although XML is not inherently evil, for multiple reasons the use of this current implantation is. First, `ext/xmlrpc` relies on the abandoned `libxmlrpc-epi`. This abandonment can be verified by scrolling through the amount of spam currently on the xmlrpc-epi-dev mailing list. That is strike one. Strike two is that PHP is currently implementing version 0.51, but the latest version is 0.54. One solution is to take control of the library and continue updates and maintenance. This is not the goal or aim of the PHP team. The proposal was submitted to unbundle `ext/xmlrpc`, which will mean that it is treated as a third-party extension, through PECL, and therefore it becomes the end user's decision and responsibility to choose to use it or not. It is important to note here that the team does not consider ext/xmlrpc useless or in need of deprecation. The API and functionality work as intended. This is merely a step to prepare for what might be next for this library or PHP regarding XML.

Don't Automatically Unserialize Phar Metadata Outside getMetadata()

Version: 0.4

Date: 2020-07-07

Author: Tyson Andre

Implementation: https://github.com/php/php-src/pull/5855

Votes: 25 / 0

Besides its catchy name, this addition to PHP 8 brings with it a much needed security update. A quick search for "php phar stream wrapper vulnerability" will return several results affecting Drupal, WordPress, Prestashop, and more. Basically a majority of websites on the Internet today are vulnerable before PHP 8. As the RFC notes, "unserialization can result in code being loaded and executed due to object instantiation and autoloading, and a malicious user may be able to exploit this."

The Proposal

Don't unserialize the metadata automatically when a phar file is opened by PHP. Make PHP unserialize the metadata only if Phar->getMetadata() or PharFile->getMetadata() is called directly.

Additionally, add an array $unserialize_options = [] parameter to both getMetadata() implementations, defaulting to the current default unserialize() behavior such as allowing any classes. (As an implementation detail, if $unserialize_options is set to anything other than the default, the resulting metadata won't be cached and this won't return the value from the cache. For example, getMetaData(['allowed_classes' => []]) after setMetadata(new stdClass()) will likely trigger a unserialize(['allowed_classes' => []]) call internally.

Backward-Incompatible Changes

Any side effects from __wakeup(), __destruct(), and so on, that were triggered during or after unserialization of metadata when the phar is loaded will stop happening, and will only happen when getMetadata() is directly called.

Index

A, B

Abstract trait method, 120–121
Arithmetic/bitwise operators, 87
Arrays, 105
Attributes
    classes, 62
    compiler/userland types, 63
    debugging, 63
    doc-comment, 61
    elements, 59
    event listener declaration, 65–67
    language construct, 60
    namespace, 62
    structured deprecation, 64–65
    use cases, 63–68

C

Casting floats, 123
Class constructor
    constraints, 102–103
    objects, 117–118
    optimized method, 102
    value object, 101
Constant dereferenceability
    class, 109
Cryptographic message
    syntax (CMS), 113–118

D, E

Document object model (DOM)
    implementation, 105–107
    interface, 107
    standard APIs, 105
Dynamic Assembler (DynAsm), 4

F

Fatal error, 104
fdiv() function, 103–104

G

get_debug_type(), 110–112
getMetadata()
    phar wrapper vulnerability, 128
    unserialize(), 128
    __wakeup()/__destruct(), 129
getTraceAsString()/toString(),
    126–127

H

Handling function
    attributes, 34
    __call()/__callStatic(), 35
    call_user_func_array(), 35

© Gunnard Engebreth 2021
G. Engebreth, *PHP 8 Revealed*, https://doi.org/10.1007/978-1-4842-6818-6

Nullsafe operator
  benefits, 55–57
  forbidden code, 57
  methods, 53
  short circuit, 54–55
Numeric strings
  arithmetic operations, 97
  arithmetic or bitwise
      operators, 96
  bitwise operations, 98
  concept, 95
  objectives, 96
  proposed solution, 96
  string-to-string
      comparisons, 98
  type declaration, 97

P, Q

PDO error mode, 88
preg_last_error_msg(), 112

R

Reclassifying engine warnings
  arguments, 46
  conditions/undefined
      errors, 44–46
  errors, 37
  exceptions, 39–44
  fundamentals, 38
  objections, 51
  principles, 47–51
  reclassification, 38

S

Saner string comparisons, 90
Short circuiting, 54–55
Stable sorting, 99
str_begins_with()/str_ends_with()
      functions, 83
str_contains function, 85
Stringable interface, 110

T

Throw exception, 121–123
token_get_all(), 118–120
Trailing commas, 92
Traits methods, 120
Type handling
  redundant types, 17–18
  union types, 15
  void/null types, 16

U

Unbundle ext/xmlrpc, 127–128
Union types
  add/remove, 20
  advantages, 14
  handling (see Type handling)
  individual union member
      allowsNull() method, 26
      coercive typing mode, 22–23
      reflection, 26–28
      getTypes() method, 26
      parameter position, 21